Janice Cappucci has recounted the sufferings of the saints as a doorway to greater intimacy with God. Aptly named, *Storm Clouds of Blessings* powerfully illustrates the reality that suffering serves the good purposes of God in the lives of His children. Sharing the testimonies of surrendered wills, trust in God's promises, and finding daily grace, this book is an encouragement to fix our eyes on Jesus and seek the things that are above as we celebrate both God's sovereignty and His goodness.

Sally Michael
Author and co-founder of Children Desiring God

The Lord gives, and the Lord takes away—blessed be the name of the Lord. How can we bless the Lord, even when He takes away? Because even when He "takes" He is giving! This is the theme of Janice Cappucci's excellent collection of true stories of God meeting real people in dark, difficult circumstances. It was my privilege to labor with Janice for five years in the ministry of soul care at College Park Church in Indianapolis. She faithfully dove into the deep end of people's misery while pointing them to a loving Savior who is sovereign over every person and event of our lives. Her book will give practical hope and help to people who feel their trials are beyond redemption. The book certainly came at an ideal time in my own life. As you read you will worship the God who has lavished us with every good and perfect gift in Christ and realize these gifts are most precious during the hard times.

Doug Pabody
Associate Pastor, Faith Bible Church, Cincinnati, Ohio

As I read the inspiring stories embedded in each chapter of *Storm Clouds of Blessings*, two thoughts kept running through my mind. First, "What a beautiful example of the biblical counseling truth that we have to *relate God's eternal story of hope in Christ to our daily story of hurt, pain, and suffering in this world.*" In chapter after chapter, story after story, Janice Cappucci does this powerfully and beautifully. Second, I kept thinking, *"Storm Clouds of Blessings* is like a narrative version of my book *God's Healing for Life's Losses.*" I'm not saying that so you go out and buy my book—honest. I'm saying it because I so appreciate the way that Janice uses *narratives of God's people to picture principles from God's Word.* If a picture is worth a thousand words, then *Storm Clouds of Blessings* is worth a thousand books on how Christ brings us hope in life's hurts.

Bob Kellemen
Author of *Counseling Under the Cross: How Martin Luther Applied the Gospel to Daily Life*

Gripping! From the foreword to the final chapter, where Janice shares her personal story of suffering and the sufficiency of the grace of God, you won't be able to put this book down. Be prepared to self-reflect on seasons of suffering from your past and to embrace those same seasons in the future with greater courage.

Gabe Turner
Lead Pastor of The Point Church, Charlottesville, Virginia

Suffering is inevitable in this broken world. In *Storm Clouds of Blessings* Janice Cappucci beautifully recounts stories of real people who found that trials were doorways to enjoying what they were made for—intimacy with the God who made them. She illustrates vividly what is compelling about Christianity. At the heart of the Christian story —the death of Jesus Christ—unspeakable good comes from horrific tragedy. And this is what God is able to do in the lives of people who look to him in the midst of their trials. Without minimizing the profound pain faced by the characters in these stories, she brings hope to those of us walking through dark seasons. Reading these stories will change your perspective on the storms of life.

Jeff Ballard
Professor of Biblical Counseling and Equipping,
Crossroads Bible College

Sufferings do strengthen us. They also provoke us to abandon our faith in Christ. Jesus clearly says that people will run away from and reject God and His Word because of trials and suffering (Mark 4:17). I have seen this battle played out in the many lives I have ministered to over the years. Through the stories in *Storm Clouds of Blessings*, Janice Cappucci provides for us examples of how people of God faithfully dealt with their suffering. Their stories will encourage you, sanctify you, and show you how to glorify God through your suffering. *Storm Clouds of Blessings* is great stuff—a very helpful resource.

Andrew Rogers
Professor and Program Coordinator of Biblical Counseling,
Boyce College

Proverbs says that "He who walks with wise men will be wise." Janice has collected the stories of ordinary people who have become wise and grown in their faith through testing. As you walk with these sufferers through their trials you will see how they became wise by abiding in the wisdom and promises of God's word and you too will grow in Christ through their example. I saw glimpses of myself and my own questions, doubts and fears coming up in the minds of the sufferers in these stories. Satan accuses us of not being really saved and of being completely unworthy of God's love and care due to our sin. He wants us to doubt God's lovingkindness and His promises. Having gone through over three years of clinical depression in two different episodes of my life, I have experienced these thoughts and doubts again and again. Through each testimony you read in this book you will be comforted by the precious promise of God's word faithfully applied in each life. Yes, Satan will seek to accuse your soul in your suffering but these stories will teach you to "… resist him, firm in your faith, knowing that the same kinds of suffering are being experienced by your brotherhood throughout the world. And after you have suffered a little while, the God of all grace … will himself restore, confirm, strengthen, and establish you" (1 Pet. 5:9-10). Read these stories yourself and share them with others so that the saints might be strengthened in their suffering.

Robert Somerville
Adjunct Professor, The Master's University, Fellow ACBC,
Board Member ACBC,
Author of *If I'm A Christian Why Am I Depressed?*

Jesus promised that in this world, His people would face tribulation. But our Lord didn't stop here, but promised, "Take heart, I have overcome the world." Janice Cappucci has illustrated that great truth powerfully with the compelling, grace-saturated stories that come to life in this volume. What the world calls affliction and disappointment are often, for the follower of Christ, streams of mercy that our great and sovereign God uses to fashion us more and more into the image of His Son. Read these stories and be reminded afresh that the suffering believer can sing joyfully with the psalmist, "It is good for me that I was afflicted, that I might learn your ways." God's grace is always good, but it's not always comfortable.

Jeff Robinson,
Senior Editor, The Gospel Coalition

*True Stories of Ordinary
People Finding Hope and
Strength in Times of Trouble*

# STORM CLOUDS
## *of*
# BLESSINGS

Janice M. Cappucci

Foreword by Steve Saint

CHRISTIAN
FOCUS

Copyright © Janice M. Cappucci 2018

Paperback ISBN 978-1-5271-0028-2
Epub ISBN 978-1-5271-0169-2
Mobi ISBN 978-1-5271-0170-8

First published in 2018
by
Christian Focus Publications Ltd,
Geanies House, Fearn, Ross-shire
IV20 1TW, Scotland
www.christianfocus.com

A CIP catalogue record for this book is available
from the British Library.

Cover design by Pete Barnsley

Printed and bound by
Bell & Bain, Glasgow.

# Contents

God moves in a mysterious way
His wonders to perform;
He plants His footsteps in the sea
And rides upon the storm.

Deep in unfathomable mines
Of never failing skill
He treasures up His bright designs
And works His sovereign will.

Ye fearful saints, fresh courage take;
The clouds ye so much dread
Are big with mercy and shall break
In blessings on your head.

~ An excerpt from "God Moves in a
Mysterious Way"
by William Cowper (1731-1800)

# Acknowledgments

"If I ever happen to fall off a cliff while hiking," I once told my husband Tom, "you have to tell people, 'She died doing what she loved best.'" I was reminded of that two-and-a-half months ago when I slipped off a wet rock while hiking and shattered both wrists. After a fun visit to the emergency room and a delightful stay in the hospital, I realized perhaps hiking is *not* actually what I love best. Because, in my anesthetized state, I found myself saying things like, "My wrists are on fire. Did you know one day Jesus is going to come back and there will be no more pain or suffering?"[1] The conversations that ensued helped me realize the thing I love the best, even more than hiking, is using words to talk about the Word made flesh—and to hear *other* people— like the people in this book—do the same. May

---

1. Revelation 21:1-5

the Lord pour out abundant blessings on these beautiful, generous, inspiring people:

Steve Saint and your lovely wife Ginny— through your example, you have helped the world understand that our loving Heavenly Father always has a good purpose and design in our hardships and calamities.

Maria Yanyuk—your courage against the Nazis is mind-boggling. Your heart-felt longing to tell the world about Yeshua, the Messiah, deserves a bigger platform than is possible in this little book. What an honor it was to speak with you and to partner with your gifted and diligent grandchildren, Elena Taube Bailey and David Taube, who patiently translated from Ukrainian, and were faithful in sharing the wonders of your story.

Wendy and Eric Su—your humility, your perseverance, your faithfulness in loving and serving "the least of these"—all these things spur us on toward love and good deeds. You are more influential than you know. I cherish our friendship.

Cheryl and Jerry Miller—you were vulnerable and transparent in showing us the long and hard process of experiencing trauma and coming out the other side victorious. Bless you for that, for your sweet and gentle spirit, and for all your work ministering to the marginalized.

The phenomenon known as Dr. Richard Ganz— you are the fuel in my evangelism tank. Your commitment and genuine love for those who may have never heard the Good News of Jesus Christ has cost you—but you press on fearlessly, willing to suffer that they may know Truth. And many thanks to your amazing assistant Dr. Amy Cameron—you were a tremendous help while you yourself were in a medical storm.

Five other truly remarkable people, whose identities were protected—you care about the people who brought storms into your life. You want to return good for evil. You pray for their redemption. That is Christ on the Cross. Thank you for your example.

Others are well deserving of heart-felt thanks. One day I expect to see dazzling, bejeweled crowns on the heads of these mentors in biblical counseling and spiritual maturity: Doug Pabody, Randy Patten, Mark Vroegop, Andrew Rogers, and all the pastors at College Park Church in Indianapolis; and the amazingly gifted Worship Arts team there who diligently prayed for my recovery; and these writing colleagues: Sally Michael, Marianne and Andy Miller, Cheryl Cecil, Becky Emerick, Charity Singleton-Craig, and Lori Ann Bachman; and Greg Pilcher, an exceptionally talented graphic designer; and these steadfast encouragers: Dawn and Terry Sites, Nancy and Rick Hampton, Jeanne Gaessler, Susan Rice, Julie Moss, Deb Weber, Don and Cheryl Bartemus, Jill and Scott Pittman, Lynn Querin, Linda Draper, Kimberly Shannon, Jeff Ballard, Mary Maley; and these saints from The Point Church in Charlottesville, Virginia who prayed and/or brought meals after my surgery: Pastor Gabe Turner, Bonnie and Tom Russman, Renee Boyle, Debbie and Lee Fletcher, Kathy and Carlos Burns, Deb and Floyd Lively, Kathy Carpenter, Melody Criswell, Claudia and Richard Ring, and Ana and Felix Galvez.

These precious people are especially dear: Tom, always eager to serve, helped me in ways I can't even begin to describe. Our one-of-a-kind daughter Natalie, and her sweet husband Sam Spoerle literally spoon fed me in the hospital. Our thoughtful son Brian Cappucci and his beloved, kind-hearted Catherine Batka sent gifts and flowers. My parents, Ron and Terry Minor, rushed to Virginia from New York to help, and my ever-encouraging siblings, Barbara Headrick, Lance Minor, and Diane Fine sent love from afar. To all of you, and all the unnamed helpers, your outpouring of kindness melts my heart—and, I'm convinced—did much to speed my healing.

Many thanks to William Mackenzie who was gracious and patient as my bones healed, to my insightful and dedicated editor Anne Norrie, and to all the good folks at Christian Focus Publications.

Grace and peace,

Janice

# Foreword

When life is hard and painful, it's easy to focus on the trial and the things we've lost. Yet the blessings I've found in the course of my life have come as a *direct result* of trials and storms. As odd as that sounds, I know I'm not alone in this— as evidenced by the book you are now holding. In *Storm Clouds of Blessings*, Janice Cappucci has brought together a collection of true stories that reflect aspects of my own—stories that refuse to let tragedy be the last word, stories that help us see God's power to transform the fiercest storms into something beautiful, something that pierces tragedy's pain and darkness with praise.

Naturally, we still experience deep sorrow and grief, but as I look back on hard seasons, what resonates most in my mind is the last line of my favorite poem: "God never gives a thorn without

15

this added grace, he takes the thorn to pin aside the veil which hides his face!"[1]

When I was five, and my whole world revolved around my dad, he was brutally speared and hacked to death by a stone-age tribe, deep in the Amazon jungle. Miles from anything we would call civilization, five dedicated, capable missionaries lost their lives at the end of a spear. Not only did this strike me as useless, it destroyed my life as a little boy.

I could not have imagined how this was a part of God's plan.

But over the next few years, these same tribesmen who speared my father and his friends became family to me. One of them "adopted" me as a son, two others became spiritual mentors and baptized me. Then, over the last fifty-eight years, thousands and thousands and thousands of people have told me personally that God has used the death of my dad, Nate Saint, and Roger Youderian, and Jim Elliot, and Pete Fleming, and Ed McCully to inspire them to give their lives to God as missionaries, pastors, youth leaders, and filmmakers.

There was no missing the lesson: *God wanted me to know something very specific about Him—that He is a God of purpose and design.* Words cannot begin to describe the strength I derived from knowing God this way—or how absolutely essential it would prove to be in the trials that would follow.

---

1. "The Thorn" by Martha Snell Nicholson. See page 22.

The next trial stormed in on a day that should have been one of pure sunshine and joy. Seventeen years ago, our family had gathered to celebrate the return of our twenty-year-old daughter, Stephenie, who had just completed a tour with a Christian singing group. Our "little girl" was back with us and we could barely contain our excitement. But that evening, our joy turned to horror. One moment she was asking us to pray for relief for her headache, and the next her eyes were rolling back in her head. One moment we were celebrating and the next we were in the ICU, hearing the words "brain aneurysm" and "fatal." Before we knew it, we were signing papers to donate her organs to people we did not know.

Reeling from this devastating loss, it never occurred to Ginny and me that losing Stephenie might also one day become a *storm clouds of blessings* story.

Just two days after Stephenie's funeral, I was scheduled to fly to Amsterdam with two members of my jungle family to speak to 12,000 evangelists from around the world. "Grandfather" Mincaye, the one-time fierce warrior, the man who had speared my father, spoke about the death of my daughter, whom he considered a granddaughter. He confidently told the assembled evangelists that she had gone to God's place where he expected to soon follow. He urged them all to invite all the "foreigners" in their part of the world to follow the trail that Itota, the Creator's Son, marked with His powerful blood.

Just before we had begun to speak, I had learned that Chuck Colson wanted to give us three minutes of his allotted speaking time. As I pondered how to best use that time, I thought about Mincaye—how he had never really grasped that being a murderer—the thing he had meant for evil so long ago, and what had so shattered my life as a boy—God had meant for good. I asked those in the audience who had been directly impacted for good by what Mincaye had done, to please stand. I expected 200–300 people to stand. But as the message was translated into multiple languages, at least 9,000 people stood to their feet. Mincaye was confused—until I explained that they were standing to tell him that God had used his sinful past for good in their lives.

A few years ago, a pastor of a large church in Atlanta told a good friend that he was jealous of both of us because of the losses we had both recently suffered. "You're making me jealous," he said, "because God would not let these things happen unless he had big plans for you. I haven't suffered for years now and I'm afraid God has put me out to pasture." This pastor actually felt cheated because his life had become easy.

Is that absurd, crazy thinking? I think he's right. Consider this story from a young lady who attends his church: Laura Story wrote "Blessings," the best-selling, award-winning song after suffering with her husband as he battled a brain tumor and meningitis. You may recognize the chorus:

> Cause what if Your blessings come through raindrops?
> What if Your healing comes through tears?
> What if a thousand sleepless nights
> Are what it takes to know You're near?
> What if trials of this life
> Are Your mercies in disguise?

If Laura hadn't travailed alongside her husband, she could never have written the lyrics that ministered to millions. If C. S. Lewis had not suffered, he couldn't have written, "God whispers to us in our pleasures ... but shouts in our pains." If Paul hadn't suffered, he couldn't have proclaimed, "For to me, to live is Christ and to die is gain."[2] If Jesus hadn't suffered on our behalf, he wouldn't have been our perfect Savior.[3]

These truths mean more to me now than ever. Six years ago, at age 63, I could jump in my plane and fly off to ministry and adventures whenever it suited me. I could still hike the rugged trails of the Amazon with the tribal people who were my jungle family. I could use tools and manipulate mechanical parts to invent a flying car designed to facilitate remote missionary work around the globe. I was healthy, always on-the-go and self-sufficient.

Not today.

---

2. Philippians 1:21
3. Hebrews 2:10

These days, I wake up with spasms of pain and struggle in anguish to wash my face. These days, my fingers are too feeble to button my shirt. *How did that happen?*

Five years ago, I was testing a wing at the I-TEC[4] headquarters in Dunnellon, Florida, when something went terribly wrong. After mounting the wing to the car, I asked my driver to try 55 mph. That was the last thing I remember. Later, they told me the safety strap broke. The wing came out of its holder, flipped over explosively and bashed me in the head, leaving me crumpled in the back of the car, skull exposed and bleeding profusely. But the real damage was a major spinal cord injury, the result of massive whiplash. I regained consciousness in a medevac helicopter on my way to Shands Hospital, where they cut out a significant portion of my spinal column to relieve pressure on my swollen spinal cord. The world I emerged into was a deep, dark cave of indescribable pain.

I have spent the last five years being nursed, bathed, wiped and fed by my precious and willing wife, Ginny, who now protects me as I used to protect her. Life without her 24/7 help would be unthinkable.

But I'm not in despair and I'm not depressed. *How can that be?* How is it that I wake up in the night thanking God? How is it that I find myself singing as I struggle to walk on my treadmill? I'll

---

4. http://www.itecusa.org/

tell you how. I have found sustaining truth in these time-tested words: "God hath seldom used, whom he hath not first, sorely tried.[5]" I want to be used.

In faith, I am thanking God for how He might use me. I'm hopeful, not because I'm so qualified, but because I remember the poem and the *absolute wonder* of the pinned-aside veil. I remember what suffering has revealed to me in the past—that God is a God of purpose and design—and as such, *He never wastes a hurt.* Experience has taught me that suffering almost certainly means something unexpectedly good is about to happen—and I want Him to use my *dependence and weakness* to accomplish more than when my good health and independence made it *easy* for me to fly, and speak, and invent, and teach.

Through all these stormy seasons—losing my beloved father, our precious daughter, my health—I am learning to trust in God's purposes, even though some, I'm sure, are yet to be revealed. As horrible and heart-breaking as these trials have been, I would not undo them if I could. We are beginning to see God's purpose in Stephenie's death—in my own heart change and in the way people now respond to me. I now realize that every person is as precious to God as Stephenie is to Ginny and me. Losing Stephenie is transforming my heart, helping me see the world more like God sees it.

---

5. An anonymous saint of old.

As Ginny and I consider God's providence in our trials, one thing is obvious: Our wounds and scars are a source of courage and stamina to others. My wounds are still somewhat open and my speaking schedule is only a fraction of what it used to be, but when I speak at conferences, the person introducing me usually emphasizes my achievements, but when I am finished, those who line up to shake my hand do so not because of what I have achieved *but because of what I have suffered.*

Think about that—*our scars give courage and stamina to those who still have wounds.*

But what if *you* are the one in need of courage and stamina? What if every day brings fresh wounds, depleting your will to press on? If you are in the muck and the mire of a hard struggle, take heart. *Storm Clouds of Blessings* is for you. The stories Janice has collected here ring with this truth: pain need *not* lead to despair or bitterness. Our ever-wavering, ever-rebellious hearts would have us believe otherwise, but God has something much sweeter for you—something lovely and healing and redemptive.

That thought may seem beyond belief right now. But as each chapter of *Storm Clouds of Blessings* unfolds, you may find your heart releasing its white-knuckle grip on your vision of what your life *should* look like, and at least tentatively welcoming God's plan.

I know this is a lesson Janice has learned herself, not only from her own trial—you can read her story of storm clouds and blessings in Chapter Eight—but also from her work as a biblical counselor.[6]

So delve into these *Storm Clouds of Blessings* stories with a sense of eager expectation that God will do a wondrous, soul-mending work in your trials, till one day you too will proclaim, perhaps through tears, that suffering really is His mercy in disguise.

Steve Saint

Author of *End of the Spear, Walking His Trail*
and *The Great Omission*

---

6. All of the stories in *Storm Clouds of Blessings* are shared with permission. None are counseling cases.

I stood a mendicant of God before His royal
throne
And begged Him for one priceless gift, which I
could call my own.
I took the gift from out His hand, but as I would
depart
I cried, "But Lord this is a thorn and it has
pierced my heart.
This is a strange, a hurtful gift, which Thou hast
given me."
He said, "My child, I give good gifts and gave My
best to thee."
I took it home and though at first the cruel thorn
hurt sore,
As long years passed I learned at last to love it
more and more.
I learned He never gives a thorn without this
added grace,
He takes the thorn to pin aside the veil which
hides His face.

~ "The Thorn," by Martha Snell Nicholson

# Introduction

Back when my summers consisted of all things sand and surf, my siblings and I would often see a younger child in despair over a sandcastle ruined by the ever-crashing waves. We'd kneel and start digging, telling him what we'd learned the hard way: you must spend at least as much time on your "levee" as your castle. Now that I've lived long enough to see *adult* sandcastles washed away in an instant, it occurs to me how apt a metaphor the beach is for life. We love the beach—and the creative spirit in us compels us to dream and to build. And yet, those merciless waves repeatedly damage our sandcastles.

But imagine this: what if the crashing waves deposited not just foam and seaweed but long-sunken booty from an ancient pirate ship laying just off-shore? When gold and precious stones came sweeping ashore, would anybody care about protecting the sandcastle? Only the ones with no understanding about what is truly valuable would still be crying. The rest would be shouting and leaping for joy.

Looking back, I can point to times when I acted like that young child, despondent over the loss of a sandcastle when treasures innumerable were being poured into my lap. I'm not saying that the losses were insignificant, or that I should have squelched legitimate grief, but rather that to focus solely on the loss blinded me to the treasure that God wanted me to recognize and enjoy, even in the midst of trials and hardships.

The treasure is simply this: To have our senses so heightened and our attention so focused that we come to grasp—like never before—what God has been saying about Himself in the Scriptures all along. That famous sufferer Job put it like this: "I had heard of you by the hearing of the ear, but now my eye sees you."[1]

What is Job describing for us? Somehow, these light-bulb moments involve not just our minds, but *our senses*. "The Bible insists on using sensory language" writes Timothy Keller in *The Prodigal God*,[2] "...It calls us to 'taste and see' that the Lord is good, not only to agree and believe it."[3]

---

1. Job 42:5

2. Timothy Keller, *The Prodigal God* (Riverhead Books, 2008), p. 121

3. Jonathan Edwards said, "The difference between believing that God is gracious and tasting that God is gracious is as different as having a rational belief that honey is sweet and having the actual sense of its sweetness." From his sermon "A Divine and Supernatural Light" (www.apuritansmind.com).

This fresh and enlarged understanding of who God is changes us—specifically it makes us more like Christ—because, as Paul taught the Corinthians, when we contemplate the Lord's glory, we are transformed, by degrees, into His likeness.[4] As somebody paraphrased it, we become what we behold.

Personally, it helps me to see mere mortals dig into this matchless treasure awaiting them at the threshold of loss. My hope and prayer is that this collection of true-life stories will *"pin aside the veil which hides His face"*[5]—the veil that prevents us from seeing treasures in trials.

Each story in *Storm Clouds of Blessings* magnifies intimacy with God our Maker as the treasure that breaks forth out of tragic and heart-breaking loss.

We were made for this, and our souls languish until we find it.[6] Fortunately for us, it is God's *delight* to reveal Himself to us. From Genesis to Revelation, the great I AM[7] reveals Himself as Redeemer, Healer, Deliverer, Defender, Provider, Father, Savior, King and Lord. On every page, God demonstrates that He wants us to know Him, His character, His great love for us, His care and concern over the minutiae of our lives and His power to

---

4. 2 Corinthians 3:18

5. "The Thorn" by Martha Snell Nicholson

6. Credit here goes to Augustine, as this idea is a paraphrase of his famous quote: "Thou hast created us for Thyself, and our heart is not quiet until it rests in Thee."

7. Exodus 3:14

bring about whatever is best for us. Most of all, He wants us to know the free gift of eternal life, the forgiveness purchased for us by His Son Jesus.

But in our fallen state, this is not what we want at all. We want to be left alone. We want to be self-sufficient. We want pleasure without pain, gain without loss. If we look to God at all, it's to be a dispenser of these pleasures so we can go on our merry way—without His interference. But that is the path of destruction, and our loving God is always working to deliver us from that. How does He do it? To be sure, He often draws us with cords of loving kindness, for His kindness is meant to lead us to repentance.[8] Other times, however, He uses hardship. This too is a kindness, though few of us see it that way at the time. We forget that the psalmist said, "I know, O LORD, that ... in faithfulness you have afflicted me."[9]

*But how,* we ask ourselves, *can an ordinary person like me see God's faithfulness in the midst of affliction?* Honestly, the idea strikes me as impossible—until I remember some inspiring stories—stories from the Bible or from the lives of the Puritans or, more recently, from the lives of Joni Eareckson Tada, Hannah Whitall Smith, Steve Saint or Jerry Bridges. When I read about the "fruit of affliction" in their lives, I am strengthened for the battle—not because they inspire hero worship, but because in their trials we see God doing what He loves to do: fortify His

8. Hosea 11:4; Romans 2:4

9. Psalm 119:75

people by revealing Himself—specifically, aspects of His character that they would have otherwise known only in an abstract way. [10] In them we see God blessing "with a 'grace given' in the circle of 'grace denied.'"[11]

Every generation needs to discover such stories. Consider this advice from Puritan biographer Benjamin Brook:

> Of all the books which can be put into your hands, those which relate the labors and suffering of good men are the most interesting and instructive. In them you see ... religion shining forth in real life, subduing the corruptions of human nature, and inspiring a zeal for every good work. ... Such books are well calculated to ... fortify you against the allurements of a vain

---

10. Before he became the Apostle Paul, Saul knew of Jesus in an abstract way. And then in an example of being afflicted while simultaneously receiving a revelation of the Divine's character, he was blinded as Jesus revealed Himself in a totally new way—as Lord! But that was only the beginning! In the days that followed we can imagine Paul coming to realize that following Christ would mean trading a life of great privilege, honor and prestige for persecution and hardship—significant losses for a man of Paul's stature. Yet, of this he later wrote, "Whatever gain I had, I counted as loss for the sake of Christ. Indeed, I count everything as loss because of the surpassing worth of *knowing Christ Jesus* my Lord. For his sake I have suffered the loss of all things and count them as rubbish, in order that I may gain Christ and be found in him ... *that I may know him* ... and may share his sufferings..." (Phil. 3:7-10, emphasis added).

11. John Piper, Future Grace (Multnomah Books, 1995) pp. 66-67.

world... and to educate your souls for the mansions of glory.[12]

Brook's words, "the allurements of a vain world," bring us back to where we started—on the beach with powerful waves, inadequate levees and crumbling sandcastles. What will we do when the inevitable waves wreak havoc and create loss in our lives? Oh, that the Lord will use *Storm Clouds of Blessings* to give us *eyes to see Him* in the midst of adversity, that we may be like children at the shore braving the tide and filling our buckets with treasures untold.

---

12. John Piper, *The Hidden Smile of God*, (Crossway Books, 2001) pp.10-11.

# Dedication

Growing up in the home of Ron and Terry Minor meant being surrounded by encyclopedias, newspapers from distant cities, scientific journals, nature and travel magazines, and stacks of books from our delightfully long trips to the library.

It meant discovering that amongst the photos in our family albums, our sweet mother had thought to preserve our best elementary school essays, the blue ribbon for comedy surely going to my younger brother Lance for this depiction of life with me and our two sisters, Barbara, and Diane: "I have a little sister and she is five. My two other sisters are in their teens and boy do they bother me and laugh at me when I do dumb things, but when I get bigger what do you think I'm going to do to them?"

But most amazingly, growing up in the Minor household meant that reading was valued even more than household chores. Of course, in a home with four kids, we were called at times to trade a book for a broom, paint brush, or wallpaper scraper. But as much as our parents modeled cleanliness, order, productivity and team work, time to read was also cherished and protected.

Thank you, Mom and Dad, for all the ways you modeled for us a love for the written word. With deep gratitude, I dedicate this book to you.

# 1.

# I AM the Messiah

It was such a simple gesture—the way the middle-aged woman working there by her front door beckoned the two girls over—but after being rejected and pushed away by so many others, it was just enough to kindle a flicker of hope. In the past two years, Maria and Valya had seen so much hatred and experienced so much loss, it almost seemed foolish to hope, but seeing this woman's welcoming demeanor, it just seemed possible that she was the answer to their prayers.

Besides her threadbare coat and worn-out shoes, prayer was practically the only thing Maria had left. After a year-and-a-half of hiding in the forest, the girls, their father, and nine others from their village had been betrayed one final time, leaving Maria and Valya orphaned, weak with hunger, and lost. Their hunters had been relentless, bribing the Ukrainian townspeople, determined to find every Jew that hadn't been previously herded into the ghettos and slaughtered.

Day after day of running and hiding, and scrounging for food, and trying to stay warm had so preoccupied her mind that Maria could hardly comprehend what had happened to her family—her delightfully tranquil, loving home, their routine of going to school, doing chores and—of the highest priority—going to synagogue and learning to pray. With a rabbi for a grandfather, and parents who were passionate to pass along their love of God, the Weinstein children—Maria, age 11, Valya, 8 and Motel, 13, devoted a good portion of their days to learning the Scriptures, hearing about the promised Messiah and awaiting His coming.

It had all been so comfortable before the Nazis came. Maria's father, a respected man in the community, ran a popular grocery store and the family enjoyed warm, supportive relationships with their neighbors, Jews and Gentiles alike. But then, in September 1941, Radekhiv, Poland became the latest in a string of towns where suddenly, inexplicably, everyone was supposed to believe that Jews were sub-human, the enemy. The Third Reich, with its dreams of Aryan supremacy, began a comprehensive, multi-step plan to rid the Fatherland—and beyond—of all Jewry. It all started with a wide-spread campaign of so-called "resettlement."

For Maria's family, and all the other Jews in Radekhiv, that meant a mass evacuation to the nearby village of Luboml. Behind barbed wire and beyond the hearing of the armed guards, they talked about what was happening to them and around them. Someone said that thousands of Jews had been gunned down in Kiev, in the Soviet Union. But that was five hours away, far enough away that they believed the Germans' assurances that they'd be safe.

Isolated in the ghetto, they did not know that what was happening in Kiev was just the tip of the iceberg. Germany had just launched "Operation Barbarossa," a massive invasion of Russia—an operation so immense it was unprecedented in military history. Everywhere the German military went, they were followed by the "Einsatzgruppen"— literally "task forces"—that functioned as mobile killing units. Their mandated targets were civilians—Jews, gypsies, the disabled, the mentally ill and a host of others. Their absolute brazenness and the apparent ease at which they committed their crimes boggled the mind. Everyone wanted to know: How could they do what they did—and do it with such demonic speed and efficiency? One factor in their "success" was avert-your-eyes kind of ugly: wherever they went they found a ready supply of locals willing to volunteer their services as informants, fellow gunmen, or both. Nobody could claim Germany had cornered the market on hatred and evil.

Unbeknownst to those in the ghetto, similar atrocities were being committed much closer to home. The Germans had recently seized the city of Lwow, on the border between Poland and the Ukraine, just an hour southwest of Radekhiv. It was the munitions factory they wanted, and they found it easy enough to man the factory with Jewish slave labor. The concentration/labor camp built there, known as Janowska, became the place where the Nazis conducted early experiments in methods of mass murder—namely "gassing vans" that piped exhaust fumes back into a tightly sealed, packed van.

Like millions of others all over the continent, Maria's life had become almost unrecognizable. Her questions mounted one on top of another, unanswered—unanswerable. What was so despicable about being Jewish? Were they really going to be safe? If the Nazis didn't plan to kill them, why were they crammed together behind barbed wire? And then, turning her palms and eyes heavenward, this question: What should I do, Lord?

The thought that entered her mind pierced through the fog: *Get out. Tell your mother. Try to get everyone out, but no matter what, get out.*

Maria's wheels started spinning. Her father was already on the outside, having purchased permission to run his store during the week. She and Valya approached their mother. "No, I can't," she said. "Your brother is too afraid. But you and Valya go." Hastily, she had the girls change into plain green and brown, knee-length, Ukrainian-style dresses and don their *hustuchki*—the white head scarves that were standard for Ukrainian (but not Jewish) girls. Perhaps the guards would notice these things, not their curly, dark brown hair or their accents, and think they didn't belong in the ghetto. Then, blessing them, she urged them to go.

Later, they could scarcely believe that the guard believed them when they denied being Jewish. "I was delivering milk to some lady," Maria said. And with that deception, they were out. But where to now, especially without their father? With heavy hearts they schlepped toward the store, hoping they'd cross paths. When at last they saw him, they fell into his arms, pouring out the story of their escape. Together, they wept, knowing their family would never look the same.

At the time, Maria thought things couldn't get worse. But now, after a year-and-a-half of hiding in the forest together—having survived a brutal winter and several close calls with the Nazis—the group had been cornered. Before, they had always eluded capture. There was the time when, after hiding in a church basement, Maria's father got word from a church member: "Someone from town saw your group leaving; the Nazis will be looking for you tonight."

Then there was the time that two Nazis got distracted, arguing with each other about what to do with the girls—should they be shot along with their father, or not? The debate turned physical, creating a sliver of an opportunity for the three Weinsteins to run like the wind.

Frustrated, the Nazis created an ambush. As darkness fell upon the Polish countryside that night in early September, 1943, they laid in wait. Hunger, they knew, would force the group to come out of hiding. When it did, they opened fire. Literally dodging bullets, Maria ran one direction, Valya and their father another. Valya felt gunfire whiz by her head, coming between her and her father. The next thing she knew, her father was reaching over, pushing her down into a ditch. That push—the last time she would feel her father's touch—had its intended effect: She was no longer a target. He was.

It was a long night of trembling for the girls, and only partially because of the cold. In the morning, feeling completely defeated and beyond any desire to hide, they took to the road, their hearts heavy with grief.

"We should just go turn ourselves in," Maria told Valya. "Everyone's dead. I don't care about dying now. Let them kill us." But Valya was afraid, and pleaded with her older sister, and so for three more weeks they searched for places to hide, licking leaves for water and trying to find food from sympathetic farmers in the nearby village. More than anything, they prayed.

Maria tried to corral her thoughts, to focus on something hopeful. Focus on the here and now, she told herself. Put one foot in front of the other. Try to encourage Valya. But, oh how her feet hurt. For the thousandth time, she longed for a pair of socks. But there was one thing to be thankful for: Over the summer, the frostbite on her fingers had healed. At one point her flesh had turned black and stank from the rot of frostbite—but now she could use all her fingers without pain. Remembering, she shuddered at the prospect of another winter in the woods without mittens.

One day, in late September, as they approached a little cluster of homes, Maria looked at her sister's torn dress and her own mud-caked shoes and thought, "No wonder everyone slams the door in our faces. Look at us." But it wasn't just the filthy, tattered clothes. For a year-and-a-half, they had had no place to bathe. Ordinarily, she would have been mortified about body odor—but now, her mind heavy with the dilemmas of survival—such trivialities didn't even cross her mind. Harder to ignore though was her hair—matted, tangled and full of lice. Even if we weren't Jews, she thought, who in their right mind would treat us like anything but mangy dogs?

But now here was this properly-dressed lady, tall and thin—with her conservative skirt and woven cardigan, her long brown hair pinned up in a bun—pausing from her work, not repelled by them, not retreating in disgust or fear, but actually beckoning them closer. The girls meekly answered her questions, then in a matter of minutes, found themselves seated at the kitchen table, steaming bowls of potato soup before them. Then it was baths with warm water, soap, clean towels and fresh sets of clothes. "You will be with us," she told them, gesturing to her husband and three children. "You will be a part of our family." And looking at each other with wide eyes, Maria whispered to Valya: "Who are these people? Did they just drop out of heaven?"

Their name was Yanyuk—Tatiana, Stephen, and their three children, Dmitri, age twelve, Zena, nine and Dorothy, seven. Four years prior, Maria soon learned, the Yanyuks had lost a set of twins in infancy. That loss, it turned out, would have significant bearings on Maria and Valya, for from the beginning Tatiana told them, "God gave you in place of my twins." Hearing it, Maria allowed herself a little sigh of relief. They don't think of us as a burden at all, she thought. They actually want us here. But the thought of how this all came to be—the enormity and complexity of how God had worked things out for this family's good, as well as her own—she could hardly take it in. Even as her mind reeled, however, this news—that she and Valya were a source of comfort—loosened something—she could feel it—in her innards, deep within her chest. Something like tendrils, tendrils of angst, were starting to unravel.

And yet, because her habits of vigilance and keen observation were so much a part of her now, Maria couldn't help but notice that two extra mouths in the household meant sacrifice for every member of the family. But it didn't seem to matter. Even though the war made for scarce resources, and the Yanyuks were just making ends meet on their little farm, both parents and children—their new siblings—treated Maria and Valya, not like adopted step-children, but with astounding kindness and generosity. There was no other word for it; Maria and Valya felt cherished—as if they were the Yanyuk's own flesh and blood.

Fitting in took no time at all. Immediately, Maria and Valya began helping around the house and out in the field. The girls delighted in the normalcy of working with the others, tilling the rich, black soil and nurturing to maturity crops of cabbage, potatoes and carrots. Every night, Maria thought about this turn of events and every night was awe-struck. *This is like paradise*, she thought, *like stepping into a little piece of paradise.*

A sweet familiarity, almost like a fragrance, lingered in the Yanyuk home. Aside from the routine of chores and school, it became obvious from the very beginning that the most important thing to the Yanyuks was their faith in God. But in their prayers, Maria kept hearing something new—the name of Jesus. Maria had never heard of Jesus. "Did you know," Tatiana asked one day, "that the Messiah has already come? His name is Jesus."

This was astonishing news. Some of Maria's earliest memories were of her mother telling her about the Messiah. "The Messiah will come one day," her mother said, "Make sure you are always listening to God so you don't miss him. He will save us." *Had he already come?* Maria had to know. The only thing she knew to do was search the Scriptures. With a tenacity and discipline reminiscent of her rabbi grandpa, Maria began to scour the Yanyuk's family Bible. Almost immediately, she began to recognize in Jesus the Old Testament descriptions of the Messiah. She was shocked to see that the prophesies about Him were very clear. He would be a suffering servant. He would be born in Bethlehem, of a virgin. He would be pierced for the transgressions of His people. Just as the blood of the Passover lamb saved the believing Israelites from the plague of death, Jesus' blood would save His followers from God's wrath. "This is so obvious!" she thought. "All my life I have known about the Messiah. Now I know His name."

But it wasn't just the prophesies that caught Maria's attention—here, in these same pages that described a Messiah that fit her expectations perfectly, were narratives that could only be described as shocking. Here was Jesus, the Anointed One of Israel, reaching out to the dirty and despised, touching outcasts and befriending society's rejects. She couldn't have been more captivated. This Jesus—He didn't care about a person's nationality, or what they looked like or their past. He accepted them as they were. But in Him, they became new. In Him, they were fed, healed, cleansed and given a new set of clothes, spotless clothes, without stain or wrinkle.

The parallels were nothing less than staggering. Here was her life, in black and white. Here in this home she lived—warm, nurtured, beloved, protected and clean—because of a family who knew Him, loved Him and longed to follow His example.

Here, she also realized, she must prepare herself to tell her own people what she had miraculously come to know: the Messiah has already come, and His name is Yeshua—the Hebrew way to say Jesus.

Each day in the Yanyuk home, the memories of the trauma she and Valya had endured receded to the back of her mind. Of course they both still grieved terribly over the loss of their family, but the care and compassion being poured out on them acted as a healing balm. Every day, little things filled her heart with gratitude. Kneeling at a bucket that Stephen had filled from the well in town, she plunged her hand in deep, and, indifferent to how it ran down to her elbow, scooped up a handful of clear, cool water and drank. To think—only a few months ago, as evening fell, they had carefully laid out their *hustuchki* amongst the bramble and spiders' webs to collect the morning dew, and when that wasn't enough, had made their way to the nearby swamp, where they would sip reluctantly and tentatively from that murky, slimy water. *How in the world,* she wondered for the hundredth time, *did Valya and I ever survive that?* And for the hundredth time, the answer came: *Only by the hand of God— only by His intervention, from beginning to end.* Feeling suddenly parched, she leaned over the bucket again and scooped up a second handful, and a third. Clean water—to drink, to bathe in, to cook actual food in—such a simple, splendid joy!

But it was more than the water. When she awoke every morning to the aroma of pancakes or biscuits, she remembered the crumbs they begged for, and the fear that hovered over every interaction with the villagers. Silently, she thanked the Lord—the Lord Jesus—for her new family. Every day, she marveled at this new life and all the protection, provision, and acceptance that came with it. The only thing that lingered—and she hated that this was true— was a sense that she and Valya were still in danger. It was a habit she was finding hard to break— looking over her shoulder, trying to be invisible. Whenever there was a knock at the door, she found herself clutching Valya's hand. It just seemed hard to believe that somebody hadn't blabbed. Then one evening, about three months after they had been taken in, ominous sounds outside the Yanyuk home all but convinced Maria that their time was up.

It all started with the sound of boots—heavy, swift, numerous; then their voices—tough, proud and imperious. Hearing this, the children instantly screamed and huddled together behind their mother. *This is it,* thought Maria. *They know.*

Shouting menacing slogans, a platoon of Nazi youth—all blonde, muscular and angry—barged into the house, shoulder to shoulder, crowding Tatiana and the children to the corners. Maria found her eyes fixed on their side-arms. How often had she closed her eyes at night, only to be haunted by visions of men just like this, bearing weapons just like this?

"You are harboring Jews," one of them barked at Tatiana. "You know what will happen to you." Tatiana did know, and so did her children. As soon as Maria and Valya had arrived, Tatiana and Stephen had a private discussion with Dmitri, Zena and Dorothy. They should know the risk. Would they all be willing to do this thing—despite the mandatory death sentence? Without a doubt, they all said. It was the only thing to do. And now, here they were, the risk a reality.

The leader, a man of about twenty, with evil in his eyes, looked right at Maria and said, "Do you know who killed your father?"

Startled, Maria managed to shake her head and eke out a tiny "No." But that was not true. The minute he asked the question, she knew her father's murderer was staring her in the face. But she dared not reveal that. "If I let on," she thought, "he will shoot me on the spot." She tried to affect a blank expression, but all the while the voice in her head cried out, "Jesus, save us!"

The young man turned again to Tatiana. "Give them up or we will kill your entire family."

Maria and Valya gasped, but Tatiana squared her shoulders, widened her stance, locked eyes with the youth and said, "These are all my children."

"You are all going to come with us," he said. "You are breaking the law."

"No," Tatiana said, tilting her jaw forward a notch. "They are all mine. We are not going anywhere."

For a few seconds, nobody spoke. It seemed like nobody even breathed. Tatiana's steely gaze was unwavering. She looked absolutely fierce. Maria could not believe what was transpiring before her very eyes. Would this armed soldier, with fifteen strong reinforcements, actually back down from an unarmed woman? His faced reddened. Was it rage or shame? Maria wasn't sure. He clenched his fist, released it, made a slight movement toward his gun and then let his arm drop. Then, breaking eye contact, he grunted something unintelligible to his men, and motioned them all out the door.

Apart from her father, Maria had never seen anyone act so courageously in all her life. As Tatiana turned away from locking the door, all five children—and truly they were all her children—

rushed toward her, engulfing her with hugs and immersing her in tears.

For weeks and months afterwards, Maria replayed the events of that night in her mind. To see with her own eyes this whole family put their lives on the line for her and Valya—no words could quite describe the effect it had on her—except to say that her heart felt like a well-tilled garden, a place prepared for good seeds. Of one thing she was certain: Living with this family made her want to grow—to obtain whatever it was that made these people who they were.

Immediately after the showdown, Maria and Valya decided that they wanted to accompany the others when they went to church. She became like a sponge, soaking up everything they taught about Jesus' life and death, the meaning of the cross, her new life in Christ and the rich blessings that come with belonging to Him.

Most of these things filled her with deep gratitude. And yet, one agonizing question pressed heavily on her mind—how could she reconcile what she was learning about God's forgiveness with the way she felt about the Nazis? Despite all the good surrounding her now, she felt like there was a barrier, a wall that kept her from fully appreciating it. In those moments when she was reminded of her parents or her brother, or their hardships in the forest, she felt an acidic gnawing in her gut. "Lord," she prayed, "I know you don't want me to be bitter. Please help me!"

The answer came for her at church. It seemed like everything they read and talked about was designed to paint for her a vivid picture of Jesus' suffering at the hands of men. "Lord," she said, "You have suffered so much more than I. You were betrayed by one of your close friends. You were humiliated in a way that I never have been. You endured pain that I can't even fathom. And yet you forgave! Even when you were hanging on the cross, naked, you prayed that the Father would forgive them. Lord, you have forgiven so much. Who am I to not forgive?"

The more Maria pondered these things, the more gratitude began to crowd out bitterness and resentment. In fits and starts, she was starting to learn that those poisons could not co-exist in a thankful heart. And how very much she had to be thankful for—not just the amazing blessings of her new family, but for how this trial had changed—no, not just changed, but enriched—her life. It was an odd thought—to realize that without these losses, she may have never come to know the Messiah. Would she have had ears to hear the truth otherwise? Would her heart have been so tender? Would she have had the eyes to recognize the Messiah, given any other set of circumstances? She couldn't say. But one thing was certain, she must live her life in gratitude to the One who ordains all circumstances and uses them to reveal Himself.

How much—and yet how little—have seven decades changed Maria's life. When she ventures outside now, it's not with a sense of threat from the Nazis, or even from the communists who outlawed religious expression throughout the Soviet republics after the war, but with an eagerness to walk amidst the richly fragrant flowers native to northern California.

On Sunday mornings, she no longer needs to pray for the safety of the believers who secretly gathered for worship at her house. Remembering Tatiana's courage and holy defiance had been an inspiration to her during those dark days—especially the day when she got word that Stephen, the youngest of her four children, had been arrested for preaching the gospel. *Oh, Tatiana*, she often thought during the four years he spent in a Soviet jail, *would you not be proud of your grandson's courage and conviction? Would you not have done the same and even longed to take his place?*

These days, when she glances at a photo of the Yanyuks, her eyes linger on her step-brother Dmitri, who, when they both turned nineteen, had practically begged her to marry him. "He was so good to me," she says, softly, "so very good and kind, that I grew to love him more and more every year."

When she goes to church now, and hears the Ukrainian translator, she often thinks of Valya. Without her pleading, Maria remembers, she might have given up hope and turned herself and her sister in to the Nazis. *Dear, sweet, faithful Valya*. Not long after being married, Maria had the joy of seeing her baby sister marry as well. When Dmitri died from cancer in his mid-fifties, Valya, her sole blood relative from before the war, was a great comfort to her, and continued to be a faithful witness for Christ till her death in 2006. How bittersweet it was to leave Valya shortly after the collapse of communism in 1989. But Maria's daughter Vera— along with her husband Valery and two little ones, Elena and David—had taken the first opportunity after the fall of the Iron Curtain to emigrate to the United States. Both gainfully employed, they wasted no time convincing Maria to join them in the Bay area.

So much has changed. And yet, no. Tenacity, perseverance, faithfulness—the things that helped Maria survive eighteen-plus months of hiding, the loss of all but one member of her family, the threats of hunters at the door—these are traits Maria's children and grandchildren see every day. "Even at her age," says David, "she prays that God would use her. She is always looking for opportunities to tell what God has done for her."

"My grandmother wants to tell everyone that Yeshua is the Messiah," relates Elena—who, along with David, often translates for her. "She says, 'All my Jewish friends need to know that.'"

# 2.

# I AM Present

Ninety five pounds. That's what Tracy had dieted down to after she started to suspect that her husband Hank[1] was cheating. "Everyone began asking me, 'Are you okay, Tracy? Is something troubling you? You look gaunt.'"

At 5'4" she looked worse than gaunt—skeletal was more like it. But when family and friends asked she'd say, "I don't know why I'm losing weight. I'm eating tons. It must be the triathlon training. I'm fine." Truth be told, her diet was pitiful—the bare minimum—and her mental state was just as emaciated. Every day she battled intense hunger—not just for food but for the slightest indication that Hank still found her attractive. He hadn't seemed to notice her weight loss, so one day, she asked him, "Do you think I'm too thin? People seem concerned."

---

1. Names and identifying details have been changed.

"No, you look great," Hank said. Brief as it was, the affirmation felt filling—almost as good as food. She'd chew on those words, ruminating on their significance. It had been so long since they had had any kind of intimacy, she clung to his appraisal. As she ran and cycled around the dusty trails surrounding Santa Fe, she comforted herself. *Maybe he hasn't started looking elsewhere. Maybe he does still find me attractive.*

But how to explain what she saw at the Railyard Park concert last night? It was a star-filled evening in a large park west of downtown. The crowd was on their feet, bopping and swaying to the steady tempo of the indie rock band. Yes, Hank had been drinking too much, but in the six months since their daughter had been born, they had rarely gotten out. It felt good. Their friends Jillian and Greg were with them, just like life pre-baby. *It's just what we need*, Tracy thought. *Things have been stressful, but tonight, we're free.*

At one point, Greg excused himself to go chat with a friend across the lawn. Within minutes Hank slipped his arm around both Tracy and Jillian. And when she looked over, she was startled to see Hank's left hand cupped over Jillian's breast. "It was his wedding ring that caught my eye," Tracy said. "I spun out from under his arm and lit into him."

Not surprisingly, both Hank and Jillian denied anything inappropriate. When Greg came back, it turned into a "he-said/she-said" situation. Greg listened, but in the end said, "I didn't see it, so I have to believe my wife." Frustrated and defeated, Tracy managed over the next few days to convince herself that maybe she was seeing things. Or maybe the beers Hank had that night made him careless and sloppy with his hands and arms. "Jillian was my best friend," Tracy said. "I just couldn't believe my best friend or my husband would betray me."

Then there was this frustration: "Anytime we'd argue," Tracy said, "anytime I questioned his behavior, Hank would say, "You're going crazy. I feel so bad for you. All I want is for you to be happy. You need counseling. You need meds.""

"He said it so often," Tracy said, "I started to believe him. I thought, 'I am literally going crazy.'" The path of least resistance was to push the thoughts away.

Even so, questions filled Tracy's mind. *Is this normal? Does everyone feel this way? Maybe this is what marriage is: Everyone pretends everything's okay, but it's really horrible.*

But pretending was draining. Red flags were everywhere. Besides the almost total lack of intimacy, there was the blank *Playboy* subscription card she found on the bed one day. "Let's not pretend everything is fine, here," Tracy said. "Tell me the truth. Is this yours?"

"I don't know how that got there," Hank said, feigning total befuddlement. "It's so strange.

Somebody must have broken in to our house and left that there."

She *wanted* to believe him, desperately so. That desire, coupled with Hank's frequently voiced opinions about her sanity, made her doubt her doubts, suspect her suspicions. *Some crazy person got into our house,* she thought, and moved on.

But every few months, there was something else— like the strange way Hank argued with Samantha, a woman who worked at the sporting goods company owned by Hank's father. "Hank would come home and describe their conflicts to me, and they always sounded like lovers' quarrels. 'Samantha said I hurt her feelings today,' Hank would say. 'The problem is she always wants special treatment.'

*Why? Why would Samantha expect special treatment?*

Again, Tracy thought about the close friendship she had developed with Samantha, and the way Hank had cultivated a friendship with Samantha's husband Parker. "Hank wanted to include them in a lot of our free time, so we'd often do things as a foursome," Tracy said. "Hank even convinced Parker to work for him, so now they were *both* employees at his father's company. *Why would he want Parker around the office if he were having an affair with Samantha?* Tracy reasoned.

But still, she doubted. She wished for a friend who *wasn't* in the middle of the mess—someone who might validate her suspicions without being judgmental or blaming. But since moving to New

Mexico after their wedding, she had no other close friendships besides Jillian and Samantha. The women in her Bible study were friendly enough, but how do you share something this personal with people you just met?

But she wasn't the only one in a Bible study; Hank was too. And his was led by their pastor. The thought gave her hope. *Maybe one day that will make a difference. Maybe one day Hank will hear something convicting and come clean.*

She thought, too, about home. San Diego seemed a million miles away. Her parents had such a solid marriage. *What is keeping me from picking up the phone and telling Mom everything? But I can't tell her. I never hear her speak poorly about my dad, so I surely am not going to speak poorly about Hank.*

"I think you're right, Hank." Tracy said one morning after a night of arguing. "Maybe counseling would help us. But it can't be just me. We need to go together." Hank reluctantly agreed to go, and Tracy's hopes were high, but the first one they saw couldn't see past Hank's charm. He dismissed Tracy's concerns, much to Hank's delight. "It was just the ammunition he needed to shoot down my suspicions," she said.

"This is outrageous," Tracy muttered the next day as she adjusted the straps of her cycling shoes and wheeled her bike out of the garage. "I am totally alone in this." Then, looking up to the cloudless sky, she almost spat the word. "Totally."

She let her gaze fall down to the xeriscaped lawn, a proliferating mass of yuccas, prickly pear cactus and hens and chicks, thriving on a patch of ground that seemed more rock than soil. *"How is it that they can endure this drought,"* she thought, *"when I am about to wither up and blow away?"* She spied a small clump of earth on the driveway. Stepping toward it, she swung back her leg and drove it forward. As she made contact, it exploded into a spray of sand. "I am," she said, remembering her feeble attempt that morning to read her Bible, "in a dry and weary land where there is no water."

Energy far from spent, and fueled by anger, she leapt onto her bike and took off. *God! Why do you have me in this relationship? Why is this so hard? Why can't I have a happy marriage? Isn't Hank supposed to complete me? Isn't that what marriage is all about?*

An hour later, she wheeled back into the driveway determined to make some changes. "Enough pretending," Tracy said, kicking another clump of dry earth. "I need to tell the women in my Bible study. I can't continue alone, spiraling down with my thoughts like this."

The decision was easier than the follow through, but the next time she went to her Bible study, she swallowed hard and forced out the words: "Things are not good at home. My marriage is really hard. I need prayer." Seeing their instant sympathy, Tracy wondered why she had waited so long.

Other good things started to happen. Tracy found a friend, Roberta, the first friend in Santa Fe who wasn't in Hank's circle of friends. "When I told Roberta about seeing Hank's hand on Jillian's breast, she said, 'You saw what you saw, Tracy. That was not a figment of your imagination.' At last, the validation she'd been looking for.

Then, completely out of the blue, Hank approached Tracy one night in bed. A month later, Tracy realized in that one night, she had conceived. A tiny seed of hope germinated in her heart. *Could this pregnancy change everything? Maybe a baby will change Hank's heart.*

It seemed like it might be the answer to her prayers. It was, but not in the way she predicted, for instead of the pregnancy going well, it ended in an early miscarriage. And instead of it working to knit Hank's heart to hers, the events surrounding the miscarriage did something unforeseen in her own heart—something that could only be described as a shift in the object of her trust.

"The day the doctor told me the news, I was in shock," Tracy said. "I just couldn't imagine dealing with more heartache. And in that state, I just couldn't sign the papers that described the D&C as an elective abortion. My doctor said I could wait it out at home for up to ten days and told me what to expect. When I woke up with bad cramps one morning, I knew I would miscarry that day. I asked Hank, "Can you stay home today?"

"I have an important meeting," he said.

"Later that day," Tracy said, "I started bleeding heavily. I put our daughter Lydia in her high chair and curled up on the floor."

The pain came in waves. She pressed her face against the cool of the tile floor. With each contraction, she tried to distract herself. She counted the crumbs surrounding Lydia's high chair. She scratched the scuff marks in front of her face. She tried to remember her Lamaze breathing.

"Are you okay, Mommy?" Lydia asked. She was only two but she knew her mom was in trouble. *I can't stay on the floor forever,* she thought. *Lydia's going to want out any second now.* Weighing her limited options, she dialed Hank's number.

"I pleaded for him to come home. He wouldn't. It was such a scary thing to go through all alone. I can't remember ever telling him before that I needed him, so it was eye-opening to me to see how little my suffering meant to him."

The hard reality became even clearer that night. "When we got in bed, I was crying and upset and I said, 'Hank, can you just hold me?' He sighed and flopped one arm loosely over my hip. It was so reluctant, so obligatory, it was just crushing."

The next day cast Hank in even worse light. "My parents arrived," Tracy said. "They could see I just needed someone to cuddle me and they offered to take Lydia out, thinking that Hank and I could use some time alone. I was grateful, but as soon as they left Hank said, "We've got a babysitter, let's go see a movie."

"No, Hank," Tracy said, "I'm not feeling well. I just had a miscarriage."

"No, it'll be good for you," he said. "Let's go."

So they went. At the movie theater, blankly watching a car chase, Tracy thought, "This relationship is all about Hank. It has nothing to do with me." And in that moment she felt the shift. "All this time I had my eyes on Hank. I had it so ingrained in my mind that Hank was supposed to give me that happiness. But in that crisis, when I clearly voiced my need for compassion, for his arms around me, he couldn't do it."

The next day, standing in the shower, she was reminded of how often she stood under the water trying to squelch tears. *You are fine,* she lectured herself. *You have no cause to be hurting. If you let yourself feel—who knows?—you may never be able to turn it off.*

She remembered, too, how often other thoughts bullied their way past her resolve: *Hank thinks you're crazy. You aren't worthy of your husband's care and concern. What will happen if he leaves you?*

Today however, a new voice entered the fray, her Bible study teacher's saying, "What does God's word say? Think on the truth." *I know that's good advice,* Tracy thought, *but how much of God's word do I really know? Yes, I know what the Bible says, but what am I really believing and applying? I feel like such a baby Christian.*

*I want to surrender to God, to totally trust Him, but what does that even look like?*

She vowed to do everything she could to find out. She *had* to. It was simply a matter of survival. She made a plan: to pour herself into her Bible study and to find a new counselor. *Surely,* she thought, *there's someone out there who can offer some real help.*

That fall, the women's Bible study seemed specifically tailored for Tracy. The theme: Learning to give thanks in all circumstances. Together, they read and discussed *One Thousand Gifts* by Ann Voskamp. "I started to write down all the things I was thankful for, all the little things, all the moments given to us by God. I started to recognize them as gifts and not take them for granted. It was so powerful, so good for my soul. I started to separate my joy from everything Hank was doing. The more I recognized how much God was giving me every day, the easier it was to give over to Him the expectations I had for my life."

In no time, it seemed, Tracy filled up her gratitude journal. One day, with a sense of hopeful anticipation, she wrote, "Thank you, Lord for our new counselor Kevin. Thank you that he doesn't blow off all my concerns!"

In their counseling sessions, Kevin regularly challenged Hank about his relationship with Samantha. Nevertheless, Tracy continued to see strange behavior. One night, just before heading to bed, the doorbell rang. It was Samantha's husband

Parker, standing at the door with one hand on the hand-me-down television cabinet Hank and Tracy had passed on to them. "We're returning this," Parker said.

Nearly speechless, Hank sputtered, "Oh, I ... is everything ... okay?"

"We don't want it," Parker said.

And without further explanation, he turned and left.

Tracy could hardly believe what she had witnessed. "Why would he come over here so late at night to return a piece of furniture?" she asked Hank.

"Oh," he said, "Samantha is mad at me. I guess she doesn't want any of my old things around."

*Another lover's quarrel*, Tracy thought. Mentally, she put the incident on the agenda to discuss with Kevin. "Hank didn't like Kevin at all," Tracy said, "and he'd often 'forget' a lot of our appointments. One day when he did come, Kevin said, "Hank, we both know you are in love with Samantha. Just say the words."

"I'm so sorry you think that," Hank said, his eyes swelling with tears. "I don't love her."

But the truth was too obvious to push under the carpet any more. In her solo appointments with Kevin, Tracy learned how to battle the lies circling around her head and heart. "He really encouraged me in my walk with the Lord," Tracy said. "He would say, 'You are fearfully and wonderfully made.[2] You are not crazy.' It took me a while to really believe

---

2. Psalm 139:14

that, to let that absorb, but I really meditated on that verse. But I started to believe these things: He delights in me. I am made in His image. If I am made in His image, then I am loved by Him. At that point I first grasped His love and started to let go of the anger. I started to realize maybe God has a plan in this. Maybe this is what it takes for me to see Him the way He wants me to see Him."

At one point, feeling hope for their marriage, Tracy asked Hank if they could try to have another child. Once again, Tracy conceived on the first try. "Maybe," Tracy thought, "this is God telling me things are going to work out. Maybe one day in counseling he'll confess and we'll be able to move on."

Nine months later, their son Jeremiah was born. They continued in counseling, but Hank was inexorable, and for two whole years he maintained his innocence. But gone were the days when Tracy considered her suspicions a sign of insanity. Now, instead of asking him to explain his bizarre behavior, she would calmly say, "Hank, you know, confessing to infidelity is so much better than getting caught. Do you have anything you'd like to tell me?"

"No. There's nothing I need to tell you."

"Lord," Tracy prayed on her daily runs, "please bring the truth to the surface. Please, make it so he can't deny it anymore."

One day, Tracy got a call from Hank at the office. "Tracy," he said, "I'm coming home. I need to talk with you about something. My dad will be there in a few minutes to pick up the kids."

*Is this about Hank's mom? She's been really sick. Does she have some horrible diagnosis?*

When Hank's father, Chuck, arrived, white-faced and avoiding eye contact, Tracy tried to get some information out of him, but all he would say was: "I love you and we're here for you." He swooped up the kids and in a matter of seconds he was out the door.

A pot of spaghetti burned while Tracy peered out the window, waiting, imagining.

"I have something to tell you," Hank said when he arrived. And pulling her into the den, he said, "I've been having an affair."

"With Samantha?"

"Yes."

"Were there others?"

"No, just Samantha."

*Really?* she thought. *What about Jillian?* Mentally, she set that aside. *One thing at a time.*

Looking over his shoulder, she surveyed the study walls, the collection of family photos she had hung above her little desk, wondering how today's news would alter the trajectory of their family's life together. An anesthetizing numbness settled like a cooling blanket of snow over her emotions. She'd been anticipating this moment for years, but now that it was happening, now that he was actually saying the words—*could this be real?* She turned to him again. "Why didn't you just tell me, Hank?" she asked, unruffled. "I knew it. I've been prepared for you to tell me for a long time."

"I don't know. I just couldn't tell you."

"Well, I'm going to leave the house for a bit. I don't care what you do. But when I come back I don't want you to be here."

"No, I'm going to die," Hank said, falling to the floor. "I should just kill myself."

"Please don't do that," she said. "I'm going to go."

Her external composure, though, belied competing thoughts and emotions. "I was in shock, and yet I felt tremendously validated."

In the days that followed, she learned how right she had been in her suspicions, but also that she had suspected far too little. Hank's infidelity with Samantha was only the first bomb to fall. After that came a blitz: revelations that Hank was totally immersed in the world of pornography, had frequently visited "massage parlors," and that he'd been sleeping around with a handful of women—including Jillian—overlapping for a time with Samantha. She also learned that Hank had weaved a sob story about his marriage at work, telling colleagues that Tracy had schizophrenia. And most heart-breaking of all, Hank had given Samantha a ring so they could pretend they were married, saying "I wish Tracy would die in a car accident or a plane crash so we could be married."

"That cut me to the core," Tracy said. "It wasn't enough to be out of his life. He wanted me dead. All this time I'd been centering my world around pleasing him and he wanted me dead. When Samantha told me about that, she said, "The way Hank talked about you, Tracy, I really feared for your safety."

Nothing, it seemed, could stop him—until he made the mistake of telling Samantha that she couldn't leave him. "I felt horrible for you, Tracy," Samantha said in their phone conversation after it was all over. "Hank would tell people at the office all these lies about you. I knew they weren't true. When I finally saw how mean and manipulative he was, I told him I wanted out. He said: 'You can't leave me. I'll get you fired. I'll ruin your career. Yours *and* Parker's. Then what will you do?'"

Samantha had had enough. That day she went home and told Parker everything. Early the next morning, Parker was in Chuck's office telling him things about his son that no father wants to hear.

Chuck made it clear, Hank had no alternative than to confess.

And as grateful as she was that afternoon to finally have the truth, Tracy still felt at war, her conflicting thoughts bouncing around in her head like pinballs in an arcade game.

*I've been miserable all this time,* she thought as she tossed and turned that first night. *Now I can leave him. I have biblical grounds to do that.*

*But, my kids—this is going to devastate them.*

*They don't ever have to know. I can just sweep this under the rug.*

*I can't do that. I've come so far. I prayed for God to reveal the truth. He did. Now I need to deal with it.*

The next day Chuck hauled Hank in to see their pastor. "Tell him what you did," Chuck said when they sat down. Hank confessed enough that the pastor pulled together a shepherding team of four elders and their wives. They quickly decided Hank needed extensive residential treatment for sex addicts. Hank was willing and, together with Tracy, they made plans for him to go that coming Sunday, right after Lydia's fifth birthday party.

That same day one of the women from the team came to see Tracy at home. "She was convinced that God was going to redeem Hank, and advised me not to rush to divorce, to give it time."

"And you may want to consider not telling your parents," the woman added. "Think about it. If you decide to work this out, is this something you really want them to know about your husband?"

*How can I keep this to myself?* Tracy thought. *My world is crumbling, my life is in chaos and I'm not supposed to tell my mom?* But then, taking a breath, she thought, *This doesn't feel right in my gut, but I am so messed up right now, I don't know if I'm thinking straight. I will try.*

The team armed themselves with anointing oil and asked Hank and Tracy to come in. One of the elders took a high-pressure approach and forced a confession of faith out of Hank.

"Was that real for you?" Tracy asked him as they left the church.

"No."

"I didn't think so."

"I don't believe in God."

"That is not shocking. I already knew that."

Returning home, Tracy wished the normal demands of life and parenting would magically fade away, but the sight of her kitchen table, strewn with birthday party paraphernalia, brought her back to reality. *How am I going to face all those kids and their parents? How can I pretend that we are happy?* But pretending was familiar territory, and forced cheeriness had almost become second nature. "This is such a lie," she thought as she welcomed guests, sliced cake and joined the kids in the bouncy house. *If they only knew what is going on here: Tomorrow this "great guy" is starting treatment for a sex addiction.*

The next day, the bouncy house came down, the gift wrap was tossed and Hank packed his bags. Ninety days, they said. Ninety days, in most cases. For the first two weeks, there would be no phone calls or texts or e-mails. Tracy couldn't imagine what her life would look like over the next three months. *My support system is gone,* she thought. *Jillian and Samantha are the ones I'd normally turn to, but they are a part of the betrayal. If only Roberta hadn't moved away. If only I could feel confident that it was right to tell my mom.* Then, falling onto her bed, she cried. *Why, Lord? Why do you have me so alone?*

But the second she thought it, she knew it wasn't completely true. Reaching for her Bible on the nightstand, it neatly fell open to Psalm 139.

> Where shall I go from your Spirit? Or where shall I flee from your presence? If I ascend to heaven, you are there! If I make my bed in Sheol, you are there! ... in your book were written, every one of them, the days that were formed for me, when as yet there was none of them.[3]

She could hardly count how many times she had found comfort, a deep abiding comfort, in those words. Now she simply laid her head on the pages and wept. "You are the only One I can turn to, Lord. My friends are gone. My husband is gone. I can't tell my family. There are no human arms. I don't know which way is up. It feels like my life is over. I'm just giving this to you completely because I'm in way over my head."

In that instant, a powerful and comforting presence enveloped her. "As I spoke those words out loud, I knew He was right there with me, receiving them. I felt like a veil had been lifted between us. In my spirit, I heard God saying, 'I've been here the whole time. I had to take everyone away from you for you to see it, but I am here.'"

The irony was inescapable. Here she was, more aware than ever of the uncertainty of her future, and yet more able to trust and more embraced by a sense of peace. She quickly saw that this season of

---

3. Psalm 139:7-8,16b

solitude was a gift, a time when she could nurture her relationship with the Lord and cling to Him. She began playing praise and worship music throughout the entire day, and with each song, asking for an increased awareness of His presence. Some days her prayer was simply this: "I'm not going to say anything. I just want to feel you near me."

Even so, fear and uncertainty lingered nearby, waiting for an opportunity to regain control. *Was God really going to restore this marriage? The leaders at church keep saying God will "restore to me the years the swarming locusts have eaten."*[4] *What if His plan is to redeem this loss in a different way? If so, how will I know? If we do divorce, how long will it take to renew my teacher's certification? How can I minimize the impact of this mess on the kids?*

Often, as the morning rays first tiptoed into her bedroom window, she'd take note of Hank's perfectly puffed pillow and think, "You have brought everything into the light now, Lord. I don't know how you're going to work this out, but I trust You. I want your will above everything else."

At the end of the hard days, the ones plagued by single-parenting struggles, financial stresses and efforts to sift through a cacophony of conflicting advice, she'd turn out the lights, certain that her worries would mean zero sleep. But just as her heartbeat would begin to rev, snippets of Scripture would waft like a sweet aroma penetrating the innermost parts of her soul.

---

4. Joel 2:25

Do not be anxious about anything[5]. ...

You are of more value than many sparrows[6]. ...

Consider the lilies of the field[7]. ...

God is faithful[8]. ...

Cast your burden on the Lord, and he will sustain you; he will never permit the righteous to be moved.[9]

...Though he slay me, I will hope in him.[10]

Speaking these simple truths out loud, to no one but herself and the darkness, she'd drift off to sleep.

In between, a thousand moments in between, she'd see the upheaval of her life and be reminded of a jigsaw puzzle, its pieces thrown to the wind. "All I see is brokenness, Lord," she'd say, "but I thank you. You know where all the puzzle pieces go. I don't understand it and I can't see it, but I know Your hand is in it and I know somehow You are working all of this for my good and Your glory.[11] I'm comfortable with that. I am content standing on Your foundation and Your plan for my life."

She could hardly believe these words were coming out of her. *Where was the vulnerable newlywed*

---

5. Philippians 4:6

6. Matthew 10:31

7. Matthew 6:28

8. Deuteronomy 7:9

9. Psalm 55:22

10. Job 13:15

11. Romans 8:28

*half-convinced she was crazy? Where was the baby Christian who leaned solely on human relationships? Gone. Forever gone.* Confident of this, she finally felt free to call her mom. Tracy wasn't surprised to hear that her mom had long suspected trouble in the marriage. "I've seen how he treats you," Annette said, "and how unhappy you've been. But I'm appalled to hear how bad it's been! I'd like to wring his neck!" Thankfully, her next words were an invitation to come visit. "Come and let us love on you and the kids for a while," she said.

"Why not?" Tracy thought. "The kids are on summer break. And I'm in a good place with the Lord."

It was a perfect opportunity to exercise her new muscles of faith, for Tracy's parents did not understand her delaying a decision about divorce. "Naturally, they wanted to protect me. And I understood that, but I had to tell them, 'You know, God has me in this place for some reason. I know all things come filtered through his hand before they reach us. I don't know why this is happening. But before I make a hasty decision, I want to know without a shadow of a doubt that I am in the center of God's will.'"

And so she waited. And prayed. And made a trip to the facility for a few days of group counseling. And waited some more. As three month mark neared, Tracy got word that Hank's treatment team was recommending that he receive treatment at a different facility. "They diagnosed him with some serious psychiatric problems," Tracy said, "and that they hoped three months at a different facility would help him."

"I was thankful he wasn't resistant. I thought if he needed more time—absolutely—let's do this right. Come home once you're ready."

Every time they spoke, Tracy searched for signs of change. But Hank, she learned, was still struggling with his relationship with God. "I believe in God," he said on one of the weekends allowed for a home visit, "but I don't believe in Jesus."

"Then what do you do with your sin?" Tracy asked. "Jesus is the one who puts us in right standing with God, so God can look on us without seeing our sin."

"I don't know. I just don't believe in Him."

Nevertheless, they went to church that weekend. A guest speaker gave the sermon. "If you do not believe in Jesus," he said, "then you do not have a relationship with God."[12]

Tracy was awe-struck. Listening intently and peering at Hank from the corner of her eye, she thought, *This is so cool. Here we are again, another moment where God couldn't be more tangible, more present.*

"Okay," Hank said in the car ride home, "I'm still not okay with Jesus. But I can see that God is working on me. I'm in process."

Tracy could relate. She too was in process—the process of forgiving Hank and her best friends. Once again, her thoughts collided. On the one hand: the mountain of lies, the multiple betrayals

---

12.John 14:6; 1 John 5:11-12

and the weight of knowing her children would surely suffer for years because of this. And yet on the other, this undeniable truth: God was already restoring the years the locusts had eaten. Whether or not Hank changed his ways, whether or not they were able to salvage their marriage, Tracy knew she owed her intimacy with God, and her inner strength and ballast to this trial. "I was so thankful for the ways God had met me and had shown Himself to me. And I knew that if I hadn't gone through what I was going through, then I wouldn't have had those moments with God. When you have that eternal perspective, then whatever happens in the world doesn't really matter."

It was an odd realization. For years, whenever she saw signs of Hank's infidelity, she felt defenseless, an inflatable lifeboat in a sea of torpedoes. But now, now that she knew everything, and especially now that she could see God's kind purpose in the midst of disaster, she felt protected—that God was with her, shielding her from being paralyzed by fear and destroyed by bitterness. "Whenever my mind would drift toward the future and all its uncertainties, I would say, "Tracy, focus your mind right here, right now. Are you okay? Yes, I am okay. *I can do all things through him who strengthens me.*[13] God is giving me strength for right now. In this present moment, I am okay." And when I thought about the betrayals, I would remember an article I read about

---

13. Philippians 4:13

forgiveness. It said that Jesus shed His blood for all people. And I'd say, "Who am I to stand in the way of His forgiveness washing over my neighbor?"

In time, that truth filtered down from her head to her heart, first to Jillian and then later to Samantha. She didn't know when, but at some point in the near future, she planned to call them both and have that conversation, for her own sake as much as for theirs. Front burner now, though, was Hank. He'd come home. Would things be different? Would their intensive counseling and support groups make any difference? "Complete transparency is the key," their counselor advised. "Tracy needs to have full and complete access to your phone, your computer and your schedule."

Tracy added, "If there is any indication that you are having a relationship with another woman, that's it. I can't go through this again."

Hank agreed—and Tracy prayed. "I decided that this wasn't about trusting Hank or what he was telling me, but about trusting the Lord. If Hank started lying to me, I trusted that God would reveal that to me."

As the months ticked by, and the anniversary of the big reveal came and went, Tracy started to think, "Maybe. *Maybe*." But six months later, Tracy noticed that Hank was acting strange again—distracted, distant, and—guilty.

"What did you do today?" Tracy asked one day.

"I went to the golf tournament, and then I went to the hotel," he said.

The *hotel*? Tracy just stared at him, wondering when he'd realize his slip.

"Oh," he stammered, seeing her face. "I mean the office. I don't know why I said hotel. I meant the office. I went to the office."

"Hank," she said, levelly, "can I see your phone?"

It was a new phone, and for fifteen minutes, her search seemed pointless. She was on the verge of handing it back when she thought of doing a search for the word sex. Instantly, a string of text messages popped up, each one graphic, sexually explicit, and damning. With a heavy heart, Tracy read them all, knowing with each passing second that her marriage was over.

"What is this?" she asked, holding up the evidence.

"I'm so sorry," he said.

"Once again, why do you always have to get caught? Why didn't you just tell me the truth?"

"I don't know. I'm so sorry."

"This is really sad, Hank, but you know what this means."

"I'll give you whatever you want. You don't deserve this."

"I know I don't. I can't believe you'd do this to kids. After all we've been through. We're back here."

"I don't know why I do this. I'm so sorry. I won't get a lawyer."

When she turned out the lights and climbed into bed that night, alone once again, Tracy whispered a prayer of thanks. God had made His will clear, just like she had asked. And He had given her the grace to wait, to give Hank every opportunity to change. And now, knowing that she was not running ahead of God and that she was not being driven by impulse or malice, she could proceed with a divorce with a clear conscience.

"I believe," Tracy said, "that Hank genuinely had good intentions. But without the Lord in his life, he can't change. It helps me too to know while Hank was having affairs, he was cheating on his mistress. I know he's a lonely man, that he doesn't share his heart with anyone. But I pray for him all the time and the Lord has been kind and merciful, sparing me the manipulation and nastiness that are so common in divorce."

During that same season, Tracy felt prompted to settle the issue with Jillian and Samantha. She could only imagine how the knowledge of her impending divorce was affecting them, and it bothered her. It was time for the talk. "It seemed like I could hear the angst in their voices when they answered my calls," Tracy said. "But right away I said, 'I don't want you to carry around that burden of guilt. I forgive you.'"

"It was good for my soul," Tracy said. "It was really good for me. They both cried and told me how much they appreciated me saying that. And

Samantha told me something I hadn't heard before: She realized, after everything blew open, that she had been deceiving herself for most of her life about having a saving relationship with Christ. She said: 'I grew up in a Christian home. I went to a Christian college. I majored in Bible. I lived a very moral life and even though I knew Christ died for my sins, honestly, I didn't really think of myself as sinful. But God humbled me. This thing showed me what I am capable of without Christ. It was a shock to see it—I really do need Jesus. When Parker forgave me, it was then that I really understood: Jesus has washed me clean. He forgives me. Through all this, Tracy, I have come to know the Lord. And now, for you to say you forgive me too—you don't know what that means to me. It's so humbling. Because you didn't do anything wrong, but you are the one who is suffering. You are on your own, a single mother. I feel horrible that you are bearing the consequences for my sin. For you to call and offer me forgiveness, I am completely humbled.'"

As she ended the call, marveling at this turn of events, one verse, like a liberty bell, resounded in the chambers of her mind: "You intended to harm me, but God intended it for good."[14]

"Speaking with Samantha," Tracy said, "helped me realize this is, without a doubt, exactly what I needed to know His presence—because I had always believed, in theory, what I read in the Bible, but I

---

14. Genesis 50:20 (NIV)

didn't know it was true for me personally. Before this happened, I lived, essentially, unaware of God's presence. So, just like Samantha, I needed this too, to experience His presence and His reassurance.

I carry that confidence with me every day. My life is hard, but it's good. On days when I'm really tired, I want to throw in the towel, but then I stop and say, "Look at the big picture, that puzzle God is putting together. This is exactly where I'm supposed to be. God's going to take care of me. He's going to sustain me. He'll give me strength and I'm okay.

I've learned so many lessons. I don't fear things, I don't get anxious the way I used to because I know that I'm in Him and He's in me. I am girded and protected by Him. I know that. I'm trusting that. I wouldn't have any of that if it weren't for this trial. When all this came out in the open, and for a good while after that, all I felt was shock. Now all of that is gone. I don't feel any of that anymore. Now I'm just thankful for it. It's incredible what God has done."

# 3.

# I AM Merciful

Growing up in China, Eric and Wendy Su knew what they were supposed to believe: There is no God. Religion is for the superstitious and uneducated. Missionaries are the tools of western imperialists. Whether these things were true or not, they couldn't say, only that they knew no Christians and if anyone had ever described the miracles in the Bible, they surely would have considered them fairy tales.

Never did they imagine, when they came to the U.S. to pursue their doctorate degrees, that they would meet educated people who claimed that the death and resurrection of Jesus—and all the rest of it—were historical facts. More astonishingly, these otherwise clear-thinking people spoke openly about their beliefs. Eric and Wendy felt so conflicted; the families who had befriended them—their host family and later a neighbor—were so loving and yet, at the same time, seemingly oblivious to the Sus' total lack of interest in the subject. "I just wanted a friend," Wendy said, "without all this religious stuff."

But now they were in the emergency room of a large Chicago hospital. Their nine-month-old baby girl was dying. Without a miracle, she wouldn't make it through the night. How did it come to this? Wendy wondered. The doctor she had called that weekend told her that chicken pox was nothing to worry about—"just keep her comfortable." But Janet's fever had spiked and now, somehow, within forty-eight hours, it had become life-threatening. The virus had gone systemic, causing sepsis, a secondary blood infection. When the ER physician said she wasn't sure they could save her, Wendy trembled from head to toe. And the only thing running through her mind, and Eric's too, wasn't atheist ideologies—it was something they had heard much more recently—that Jesus heals.

And so, for the first time in their lives, at 2:00 in the morning, Wendy and Eric hesitantly but fervently laid their petitions out before a stranger. "Please, God, save Janet. Don't let her die. In Jesus' name." It was all they knew. It was all they wanted. And having said it all, they both fell asleep on the sofas outside the operating room.

When they awoke three hours later, the doctor said Janet was critically stable. If she made it through the next twenty-four hours, she would live. "That was the beginning of our spiritual journey," Wendy said, "because she did survive, but she wasn't the same. Over the following year, every time we went to the doctor we received a worse diagnosis."

"Over the next twelve months," Eric recalled, "she stopped saying "Momma." She stopped clapping and waving bye-bye. Instead of reaching milestone markers, she was regressing. Then, just before she turned two, she started having seizures." The chicken pox had probably caused encephalitis, the neurologist said. It was precisely what Eric and Wendy had feared: the virus had damaged Janet's brain.

Janet is twenty-one now, with severe mental and physical disabilities. Wearing a helmet with a plastic shield, she slumps over on the family room floor, playing contentedly with a stuffed animal. But to call this highly-modified space a family room is a misnomer, for it is clearly Janet's room. A Dutch door protects her from harm, as do the thick wall-to-wall gym mats. A stack of diaper boxes dominates a corner. Janet's wheelchair is nearby, as is a stash of G-tube supplies, the components needed to keep her hydrated, since she cannot swallow liquids normally. And yet, as grievous—as ubiquitous—as these signs of vulnerability, brokenness and utter dependence seem to an outsider, to Eric and Wendy, they are signs of God's mercy.

Mercy!? Yes, the word is continually on their lips—as they speak about how God not only used Janet to bring about their salvation, but how He has comforted them in their sorrow, healed their broken hearts, forged maturity, nurtured trust, bestowed peace in their anxiety and sustained them through physical and emotional exhaustion.

Not that they've always seen it that way. Getting to this place has come only as a result of grappling day by day with hardships that have impacted every aspect of their lives. Mostly, it's the routine things that take their toll—things like having to wrestle with Janet to floss her teeth, change her diaper, or to take a brief walk around the house— or to stop walking when other chores are waiting. When Janet really doesn't want to cooperate—like when it's time for her shower—she lets loose an ear-piercing squeal, flails her arms and struggles to escape. "A twenty-one-year-old has a good set of lungs," Wendy said. For all these tasks, when they need Janet to stand or walk, she must be supported, but strategically, so that if she starts to fall—which she sometimes does as a result of a *petit mal* seizure—she won't take Eric or Wendy down with her. Thankfully, Eric and Wendy say, their visits to the physical therapist haven't been for traumatic injuries, but "only" for wear and tear on their shoulders and backs. Looking at their wispy frames—skin and bones in Eric's case—another point of thankfulness comes to mind: that Janet is small for her age, and not like her older brother Leon, who towers over the rest of the family at a solid six feet.

Trial and error have helped Wendy and Eric settle into a workable pattern for managing Janet's care, but that too has taken time—time and a near catastrophe. When Janet was nearly three years old and Leon was seven, Wendy found herself pregnant again. When their son Enoch was born, they rejoiced, feeling consoled and comforted to have a healthy baby in the house again. And yet, there was no denying that a third child, with two in diapers now, meant being stretched even further, physically, emotionally and spiritually. When Enoch was three months old, Wendy's immune system took a nose dive, resulting in a kidney infection and sepsis so severe that for six days, she teetered between life and death. It was startling. When Wendy recovered, the first thing the Sus did was put themselves in survival mode—only the essentials, giving first priority to reading and studying God's Word.

A lifestyle of "only the essentials" has meant sacrifices, too, for Janet's brothers. Leon, now in medical school, loves spending time with his little sister and helping with her care; but when he was in junior high, Janet's disability meant that he wasn't able to join the basketball team. "From the standpoint of time and energy, we knew we couldn't manage driving Leon to and from practice every day," Wendy said. Enoch too, is well aware that getting one of his parents to sit down for a chess match is a low priority compared to getting Janet walked, hydrated, changed, bathed or fed.

Of course, nobody in the family finds leaving the house a simple matter. "We can't just decide spontaneously to run errands or go out for dinner as a couple," Wendy said. "If we want to have respite care, it must be arranged well in advance, and if the one nurse who has been trained for Janet's care is not available, we don't go. It's just too time-consuming to try to re-train new care-givers every time we need to go out."

When they speak, however, about the road they've been on, their focus is not on these things. Without trying to sugar-coat the hard realities, they are quick to point out that these difficulties—the nitty-gritty details, the way-too-personal care needs that assault the senses and leave the uninitiated aghast—these are not the whole story, not by a long shot—not when they look at the trajectory they had been on and the "vain and meaningless life" they would have lived, had it not been for Janet.

"Before Janet was born I had so much selfish ambition and vain conceit," Eric said. "I was in a post-doc program at a hospital affiliated with Harvard. It was supposed to be an atmosphere of collaboration in the name of medical advances, but so many of our interactions were colored by strife and professional jealousy. Because of my pride, I didn't have a very good relationship with my professor. I thought I was better than he. So when my fellowship money ran out, he wanted me to leave. I was humbled. For the first time I realized I am not what I thought I was. I began to question my attitudes and to think critically about the darkness and hopelessness that I was a part of at work."

Painful as that experience was, it prepared him for the trial with Janet. "I would have lived a pagan life if we had healthy children." Eric said. "My heart was so hard. It had been twelve years since our host family had first spoken to us about Christ, but I had no heart for the Bible. My life was about pursuing worldly things and I was blind to my own sin. But the Lord did have mercy on us. He was patient. When we moved to Chicago, the Lord gave us a Christian family in our neighborhood that reached out to us and invited us to a Bible study. I wish my heart was not so hardened that I could have believed before disaster fell on me. But the Lord used all those disasters—job and family—to humble me. People like us—we are from an atheist environment. And the sinful nature is so deeply rooted. It took a long time and a lot of discipline to uproot those things. It is God's mercy. He says: 'Those whom I love, I reprove and discipline.'[1] It is God's mercy."

Eric and Wendy see God's mercy in other aspects of the trial too: in how the truth about Janet's condition emerged so gradually, in giving Janet a sweet and pleasant temperament, in His directing them to a Bible-believing church, in giving them the grace to trust Jesus for their salvation there, and for their church friends who brought countless

---

1. Revelation 3:19

meals and babysat long hours during Wendy's difficult recovery from sepsis. Surpassing all of these things (with the exception of their salvation), the Sus see God's mercy is the way He gave them a profoundly different and deeply healing perspective about life with Janet. "After Janet started having seizures," Wendy said, "we came to the end of ourselves. We realized we couldn't do anything to help her. We just handed her over to Jesus. We were baby Christians and all we wanted was to see Janet healed. The hardest thing was she was born normal. We had dreams for her, like all parents do. But she wasn't developing. My heart was heavy with grief—worse than if she had died, I felt. If somebody happened to mention walking their daughter down the aisle, I would weep. One day, after hearing some women laughing, I thought, I don't know how to laugh anymore."

And that's the way it was for two years. But then they heard about a family retreat held by "Joni and Friends," an international disability ministry led by Joni Eareckson Tada, who has been a quadriplegic for fifty years. "That retreat was the turning point of my healing," Wendy said, "to hear Joni say that Jesus wants to heal our broken hearts—it was life-changing—because my sole focus before was on Janet's physical healing. Also, Joni helped us to think about our time on this earth as just temporary—that we're just sojourners, passing through. It was exactly what we needed to hear. God used these truths to bind up our broken hearts. If we had missed hearing about that retreat, our lives would not have been the same."

Eric agreed. "The healing of our hearts and the salvation of our souls is God's main concern. Physical healing can be a sign, it can be a blessing. But it's not the ultimate goal. Those of us who know the Lord will have new bodies in eternity."

"One Sunday after that retreat," Wendy recalls, "I realized—through a song—that God had healed my heart. We were singing 'I'd Rather Have Jesus.' With tears rolling down my cheeks I felt myself affirming those words in my mind, saying, Yes, it's true. If we had three healthy children we'd still be living in darkness. I'd rather have Jesus."

"Since that retreat," Wendy said, "my life is not focused on Janet getting better. It doesn't matter anymore. We have eternity. In eternity, Janet will be healed. The important thing is that we seek His kingdom and His righteousness first[2]—that we grow, mature in Christ and glorify God with our lives. How we live our life here matters in eternity. We want to think about our lives here as storing up treasure in heaven."[3]

But is having an eternal perspective all it takes? If it were that alone, if their minds hadn't been renewed in a hundred other ways over the years, Eric and Wendy might be living a kind of grinding existence—a life characterized by a doleful

2. Matthew 6:33

3. Matthew 6:20

resignation or perhaps a steely determination. But what comes out in their speech and demeanor is a sweet humility, a quiet joy and an inspiring kind of fortitude—attitudes they attribute to God's grace and the comfort and strength they've found in the Scriptures.

"Soon after we got baptized," Eric said, "I started listening to Christian radio and the Scriptures on CD in the car. I remember sometimes the tears would just flow. God's word is so comforting and so healing."

The verses that have been his daily sustenance roll off Eric's tongue. "Come to me all who labor and are heavy laden and I will give you rest," he quotes. "Take my yoke upon you and learn from me, for I am gentle and lowly in heart and you will find rest for your souls. For my yoke is easy and my burden is light."[4] I realized that Jesus was humble. He is gentle and humble in heart. That was really shocking to me. Great people aren't humble. And Jesus was great. So when I realized He humbled himself and suffered for our sins, even to the point of death on a cross—that was healing. Compared to Him, my suffering is nothing."

"Without God's Word," Wendy said, "I don't know what kind of condition I would be in or how I could have handled all our problems. Our pastor taught us that the Greek word *hupomeno*[5] means to

---

4. Matthew 11:28-30

5. In 1 Corinthians 13:7, Paul used this word in writing, "Love *endures* all things."

bear up under, to endure. When we have trials we don't just pray for deliverance or healing. We also pray for God's grace and strength to endure it."

Toward that end, one day Wendy decided she'd create a list of all the scriptures related to suffering and endurance. "Sometimes," Wendy said, "I would think, This is so hard. There's so much work. And I could feel myself sliding into self-pity. But then I'd remember reading that Jesus said when we serve 'the least of these' we are actually serving Him.[6] So I said, 'Okay, Jesus, I'm doing this for you. I'm serving Janet, serving one of the least. This is the assignment You have given me. I'm doing this for You. That's just changed my perspective—doing it for Him, for the glory of God.'"

Unbeknownst to her, Wendy's response to their family's hardship made an impression on one of her neighbors. "Look at your life," one of them said. "You have every reason to mope and to isolate yourself and yet you are the friendliest neighbor." The comment took Wendy by surprise. "I can't explain it. It's been a gradual transformation. It has to be from the Lord. 'The joy of the Lord is my strength.'[7] I don't think, 'Woe is me.' Peace and joy—that's really from the Holy Spirit. Life is not easy, but I feel joy."

Another friend, Luanne, noticed that the boys seem to have actually been blessed by their unusual home life. As a volunteer at Joni Eareckson Tada's family retreat, Luanne has an insider's perspective

---

6. Matthew 25:31-40

7. Based on Nehemiah 8:10

of the Su's family life. "Janet is a grace to that whole family," she said. "There's a noticeable wholeness with the boys—always happy to serve others while at the same time always ready to join in the fun with friends. And when they speak of Janet, their voices are full of obvious warmth and affection."

For Eric, humility is where he senses God refining his character—and not just at home. Five years ago when the pharmaceutical company underwent lay-offs and re-structuring, Eric was moved from a high-profile position in molecular biology to a service-type position in statistics. "It was impossible," Eric said. "I had no statistics background. But I realized it was the Lord working to nurture humility. I think of the verse that says, 'Do nothing out of selfish ambition or vain conceit, but in humility consider others better than yourselves.'[8] But being in statistics, I don't have to *consider* everyone better than myself. Everyone *is* better than I am."

Eric says the whole experience has been a way to learn from Christ. "Jesus taught his disciples: 'those who are considered rulers over the Gentiles lord it over them, and their great ones exercise authority over them. But it shall not be so among you. But whoever would be great among you must be your servant, and whoever would be first among you must be slave of all. For even the Son of Man came not to be served, but to serve, and to give

---

8. Philippians 2:3 (NIV)

his life a ransom for many."[9] So I need to practice that. I am in a service position; I *do* need to serve everyone. Once I know God's words and Christ's work, it's a joy to practice that. The Lord showed me the results. It's very rewarding."

The biggest reward Eric sees is the benefit for his family life. "It is the Lord's mercy that I can't be on the rat race at work," he said, "climbing the management ladder or the technical track ladder. I have a full-time job at home. God's grace has been sufficient and the job He's given me is sufficient to provide for the family. That's good enough. I am very content."

Even so—with their maturity coming at such a high price—isn't there even a *wee* part of them that wishes for a "normal" life, an easier life? Their answers come quickly. "I've thought about it many times," Wendy said. "Do I wish the doctor hadn't said, 'Just keep her comfortable,' that there hadn't been that human error? Tragedy happens everywhere. But God uses it for our good. Whenever times get hard I stop and think, *OK, without Janet, where would we be?* Without a doubt we'd be just like our peers and relatives from China—trapped by fear of death and living in darkness and despair, without hope, without joy. When I think about our old life, it's just depressing. No, we don't want that at all. We wouldn't trade places. We have found the truth. We'd rather have this."

---

9. Mark 10:42-45

Eric, too, is sure about what they've been spared. "Without Janet," he said, "I know I would be just like any worldly man, very unhappy because I would not ever be able to fulfill my selfish ambitions. My family probably would fall apart. The thing we've learned with Janet is that the greater thing to heal is not a disease; it's our sin. It's a disease of the soul, not a disease of the body. All of Jesus's miracles—healing the blind, the deaf, the crippled, those with leprosy—they represent the spiritually blind, deaf, crippled and unclean. That's the real healing. We are healed. 'By his wounds, we are healed.'"[10]

10.    Isaiah 53:5 (NIV)

# 4.

# I AM your Protector

Of all things, it was the dog that made Cheryl cry. "Rambo," their beloved Golden Retriever, had been in the family for thirteen years, a gift that Cheryl and her husband had given their daughter Dawn on her seventeenth birthday. Little did they know, as they wrestled that squirming little fur-ball into a gift bag, that Rambo would outlive Dawn or that they would come to cherish him as one of the last vestiges of her memory.

From the day of the shooting onward, it seemed that there was always something that kept Cheryl from experiencing a good, cleansing, cathartic cry. In the hospital, recovering from two bullet wounds, Cheryl was preoccupied with urgent concerns. A little baby, first of all—Dawn's boy Michael, suddenly an orphan—needed her. If she and Jerry were to have any chance of adopting their grandson, she couldn't allow herself to be distracted—especially since the other grandparents wanted him too, and the legal battle promised to be long and arduous. Then there were the horses. Cheryl and Dawn had been co-laborers, establishing and running a summer therapeutic riding program. Just recently they had formulated a plan to expand the program and open a year-round, non-profit riding center. If Cheryl was to take up this challenge on her own, every part of it—the horses, equipment and facilities, the staff and the volunteers, and of course, the riders, who depended on the therapy to treat their injuries and disabilities—would demand her attention, expertise and strength.

But beyond these responsibilities, there was something in Cheryl herself, something ingrained that told her she didn't have the freedom to be anything *but* "the strong one." Years of intervening in her parents' fights had left her with the sense that she was responsible for everyone else's well-being. So now, she hardly questioned that there was little room for grief, even as she faced the ramifications of her son-in-law's murderous rage. When sorrow did bubble to the surface, when little Michael, (now older, and now officially an adopted son) would see her starting to cry, he would say, plaintively, "Don't cry, Mommy. Don't cry!"

But now, seven years later, Rambo was in the last stages of bone cancer, his pain obvious and heart-breaking. The vet was called, the shot mercifully administered, and with his last breaths, Cheryl's sorrow broke through the dam. Memories, too, flooded her mind: the uneasiness she and Jerry felt when Dawn decided to marry Bill, the gut-wrenching grief at learning that he had been abusing her and the baby, the counseling and subsequent filing for divorce, Dawn's mounting fear at the way Bill had been stalking her, and most of all, the day that changed everything.

"The night before," Cheryl remembered, "Dawn was having dinner with friends. She and the baby had moved in with us, and she called me saying, 'Mom, Bill showed up at the restaurant, threatening me. I'm too scared to drive home alone so I'm going to spend the night at Debbie's house.' Even though she had a restraining order, and all his weapons had supposedly been taken away, she knew those things meant nothing to Bill. In fact, she had told her friends that night, 'Bill is going to kill me.' So she stayed the night and came home early the next morning."

Right after Jerry left for work that day, the doorbell rang.

"I want to see my son and see him now!" Bill shouted as Dawn cracked open the door.

"Bill," she said, "this isn't your day for visitation."

He pushed open the door and shoved her to the floor.

Immediately, Cheryl reached for the phone, but he said, "Don't you touch that phone." Dawn stood up, but he shoved her again. Cheryl headed toward them, but as she did, Bill reached under his jacket, pulled out a gun, aimed it at Cheryl's abdomen and fired. Then, standing over her on the floor, he pointed the gun at her head.

"Bill," she said, "God loves you and I forgive you. Please don't do any more."

"I don't care about your God," he said. "I want you to suffer."

Cheryl began to pray out loud. Just as she was bowing her head, he fired the gun again. "I don't know how it happened," Cheryl said, "but the bullet skimmed my head and stunned me. Now face down on the floor, I could hear everything that was going on but I couldn't move."

Dawn said, "Bill, you shot my mom. I'll do anything you say! Just let me get help for my mom!" She picked up the cordless phone but Bill grabbed it from her and threw it across the room.

"No!" he said. "You are *not* going to get help. You made me suffer and now you're going to suffer."

Cheryl heard the gun fire and Dawn fall to the floor. She heard him take a few steps and then the blast of another shot echoed off the walls.

"By this point," Cheryl said, "the baby was crying in his room upstairs. I heard Bill run up, grab Michael, and rush out the door. I thought, *He's taking the baby! I've got to get help!* I made myself stand up and I looked out the long window by the entrance. Bill saw me and turned pale. The look on his face said, *This cannot be. I just shot this person twice. She cannot be standing up.* He grabbed the doorknob to come back in, but mysteriously, the door was locked. It shouldn't have been, unless Bill took the time to lock it as he left, but God made sure that door was locked. When he couldn't get in, he turned, jumped in his SUV and sped off with the baby."

Straight away, Cheryl went searching for the phone. *Where had he thrown it?* Knowing time was of the essence, she headed for the corded phone downstairs. If she acted quickly, maybe Dawn could be saved. But when she picked it up, it wouldn't work. *No!* she thought with a sinking realization. *The cordless phone must be turned on. That's why I can't call out.*

Back upstairs again, Cheryl could hear Dawn gasping for breath and realized her best hope would be to look for help outside. *Maybe,* she thought, *I can get the attention of one of my neighbors.* She rushed out into the February cold and yelled for help. Nothing. Nobody. Nowhere. *How much longer can I remain conscious?* she wondered. *Maybe if I were to lie down on the pavement someone will see me.* On most other days, it could have been hours before someone passed by, but that day, one of her neighbors decided to do something different, and go home for lunch.

When the paramedics were lifting Cheryl onto the helicopter she told them, "You have to take my daughter first."

"No, you first," one of them replied. He did not elaborate. Intuitively, Cheryl knew why.

*Had it really been seven years since all these things had transpired?* She saw them with such clarity. And as her trickle of tears became a torrent, she hurried from the house, away from Michael's keen ears, away from death, away from the weight of being strong.

*Why am I crying like this?* she wondered as she headed for the barn. *What is wrong with me that I am crying so hard over our dog? I didn't even cry this hard over our daughter!* All she could think of was the comfort she knew she'd find in the barn. Duke was in the barn. Duke didn't need her to be strong. Duke, recently named the therapy horse of the year, was a pillar of strength himself. "I threw my arms around him and sobbed in his neck," Cheryl remembers. "I poured out my heart to him—first, about how much I was going to miss Rambo, but then I realized I was grieving over Dawn. It was a culmination of all the painful emotions that I felt over those years: the grief of missing her, plus deep sorrow for all the ways her death had changed our family."

Even though Cheryl had not expressed her grief until that point, or tuned into the way the shooting had affected her, the effects were there. "In hindsight," Cheryl says, "I can see how being shot, especially by someone I knew and trusted, made me extremely guarded. It affected all my relationships, but my marriage suffered the most." Trusting people, acknowledging her own pain, being transparent with her emotions—all those things felt too risky, too vulnerable, even with her husband.

Jerry, too, was battling dark forces. At closing time at the family bakery, sitting alone with his paperwork each afternoon, his mind would wander. Dawn was such a joyful, outgoing spirit! Her love of adventure, her dedication to the riding ministry, her accomplishments as a newly licensed pilot—she truly was an inspiration. Jerry knew that nothing could fill the chasm left by such a passionate life, but in his desperation, he turned to alcohol. "One quart of beer eased the pain a bit," he said, "but then it got to be two or three quarts. It was getting pretty bad." Soon, Jerry was speeding home from work, looking for the perfect tree to end his sorrow. "I had one picked out. As I approached it, I'd get up to eighty miles an hour." All such planning and rehearsing (and drinking) came to an abrupt end the day he saw blue flashing lights in his rear-view mirror.

Cheryl distracted herself with busyness. She threw herself into raising Michael and establishing the riding center. She maintained high expectations of herself as a homemaker too, and expected Jerry to appreciate her hard work. In her fragile and frazzled state, a few insensitive comments were all she needed to start imagining that Jerry thought of her only as a cook and maid. "Once that idea entered my mind, all I could see was 'evidence' that supported that accusation. I pulled away from him, but I told myself that he had pulled away from me.

We lived under one roof, but like roommates. I felt so abandoned—like he didn't love me anymore."

The loneliness was almost too much to bear. One day, Cheryl was in the garage with Michael, and as she buckled him into his car seat, a wave of intense longing and exhaustion swept over her. She thought about the sweet friendship that she and Dawn enjoyed the last few years of her life, her bright eyes and her love for the Lord. Turning her face away from Michael to wipe a tear, an idea entered her mind: *All I would have to do is sit here with the engine running and Michael and I would join Dawn with the Lord.*

The pull toward making a quick escape mingled with hard questions about her faith. "I knew without a shadow of a doubt that God was in control, but at the same time I didn't understand Him. I couldn't help but wonder, *Why, God, why?*" All too often, suspiciously dark thoughts crept into her mind: *God was able to protect you and Michael. Why didn't He protect Dawn?* The malicious insinuation couldn't be missed: *Your so-called "Protector" can't be trusted.*

And yet, even in this painful season, she couldn't deny that God had been working—really throughout her whole life, preparing her for this trial. In the garage that day, it was the habit, learned through years of meditating on and teaching Scripture at a Christian elementary school, which caused her to consider how her suicide would hurt others. *Oh, how selfish of me,* she thought as she reached for her seat belt, *that I would take the life of this baby and leave my husband and our other son and bring more grief on my parents. No, I can't do that.* Later, she reasoned, *I gave my life to the Lord. Now if I've given Him my life, how can I take it back and decide to end it if He's not ready for me to die?*

Still, she couldn't shake a sense of uneasiness. *How have I allowed myself to sink so low to consider suicide?* she asked. Her conscience was bothered, too, by the way she had been nurturing endless accusations against her husband. *Lord,* she asked, *how do I get out of this mess?* The answer wasn't audible, but in her mind, she heard these familiar words:

> We do not wrestle against flesh and blood, but against
> ... the spiritual forces of evil in the heavenly places.[1]

"Immediately, I knew what I had been doing wrong. I had been thinking of *Jerry* as my enemy. But when the Holy Spirit brought this verse to mind, I was reminded that my battle isn't against Jerry; it's against Satan. *He* is my real enemy. He's called the Accuser for a reason; he was always pointing at Jerry and telling me that he didn't care about me, that he was just using me to keep house. I nurtured thoughts like that and let them build a wall between us. I realized I had to take a stand against Satan, not Jerry, and when I did that—not just once, but repeatedly—that wall started to come down."

This way of thinking—evaluating her thoughts and feelings in light of Biblical principles and the

---

1. Ephesians 6:12

authority of Scripture—became for Cheryl the thing that lifted her, again and again, out of a pit of despair. But it wasn't easy, and some days it felt like that was *all* she was doing. Especially that first year, it seemed that every day she encountered another challenge related to Dawn's death.

To begin with, the shooting that day didn't end at her house. While Cheryl was being airlifted to the hospital, Bill headed to his parents' house. When he arrived, he laid the baby in his frail, sickly mother's lap. Within minutes, he went back to his SUV, where he turned the gun on himself. In the aftermath, one especially horrific and maddening detail would come to light: the gun Bill used was a loaner, borrowed just a week before—from his father.

Almost like a Biblical plague, death had now descended upon another home. Now, both families would be grieving one of their own—and both would want Michael. The custody battle that would last a year had begun. Bill's parents were too infirm to care for a baby, but they wanted their youngest daughter to raise the child. "I think they all felt like Michael would fill a void for them," Cheryl surmised. "But in the court proceedings, we learned so many things about the family that it petrified me to think that Michael could end up with them. And every Saturday when they were allowed to have him, I would pace the floor, worrying if they were one minute late."

"Some days I really struggled with resentment toward them," Cheryl said, "especially toward Bill's father, first of all for loaning Bill that gun when he knew the restraining order made it illegal for him to have one, but also because he was the one spearheading this custody battle, and he was going at it so aggressively.

"It was obvious that they felt resentment toward us as well. They were offended that we put Dawn's maiden name on the tombstone. But we knew that Dawn planned to take her maiden name again once the divorce was finalized. Also, they wanted Dawn to be buried next to Bill. I said to Jerry, 'These people are not living in reality. They are in complete denial. They're acting like this was a tragic car accident. Don't they understand their son murdered our daughter? He *murdered* her. Why would we want her buried next to him?'"

And so, with these hard feelings hanging unresolved over the custody battle, every interaction challenged Cheryl and Jerry's desire to be patient and peaceable.

"During the custody dispute," Cheryl recalls, "I would sometimes get panicky and think, 'What if they take Michael away? What if he ends up with his aunt and uncle?' Every time I started going in that direction I would say, 'No, I need to focus on Christ.' And I'd remember how Peter jumped out of the boat and walked on the water. As soon as he started looking at waves and the danger, he started to sink. But when he cried out and held out his hand, the Lord took hold of him and saved him.[2] In those moments when fear gripped my heart, I would literally hold out my arm and say, 'Lord, Jesus, help me to stay focused on you and rely on your strength.'"

Again and again, Scripture became for her like an iron guard rail protecting her from a terrifying precipice. In time, it even helped her with her hardest questions. *God says He is our protector and that we should trust Him,* she thought. *But does He mean for us to believe that my loved ones and I will never suffer harm? Is that how God defines protection?*

A well-known passage from Paul's letter to the Romans helped her develop a mature understanding of God's protection.

> And we know that *in all things* God works for the good of those who love him, who have been called according to his purpose.[3]

"When I was still teaching, one of my fourth-graders gave me this verse on a plaque. After Dawn's death, I took particular notice that it doesn't say 'some things.' It says, 'all things,' including those awful, tragic things. I realized I had a choice to make. I didn't have a choice about what happened to me and to our daughter, but I had a choice as to how I would respond to that. Would I really believe

---

2. Matthew 14:22-33

3. Romans 8:28 (NIV, emphasis added)

that all things work together for good? Would I let God use this to mold me into the image of Christ?[4] Or would I question and blame Him? Would I become bitter or angry? I told myself, 'No, that's not an option. I want to glorify God. He can bring miracles out of this.'"

As she practiced this mental discipline over those difficult months, new things started to blossom in her heart: Courage—and yes, something even better—confidence and trust. "After losing Dawn, Jerry and I prayed and we knew that as soon as we were granted permanent custody, we should move to adopt Michael. We also knew we were to move ahead with the dream Dawn and I had to open a year-round riding center. Prior to this, things stood in the way: fear of financial commitment, fear of change, fear of failure. Suddenly all those fears vanished. God showed us that He could bring us through the most difficult, tragic loss that a parent could face. That gave us the courage to step out in faith and put everything we had into raising Michael and establishing Agape [Therapeutic Riding Center]." The words she and Dawn chose as Agape's mission statement—to glorify Christ by serving others—became her compass for each day.

Cheryl and Jerry stepped out in faith then, expecting miracles, and yet, could not have imagined

---

4. Taken together, Romans 8:28-29 help us understand God's good purpose in trials—that they would make us more Christ-like. "For those whom he foreknew he also predestined to be conformed to the image of his Son, in order that he might be the firstborn among many brothers." (Rom. 8:29)

they'd ever hear this astounding news: Within a few days of the shooting, Bill's family reached out for answers about matters of faith. "They were all shaken to the core," Cheryl said, "and they called one of Bill's old friends—a man named Mike who used to party with Bill but now ran a small ministry in town. They said, 'Mike, we have so many questions. Would you come talk to us?' They talked for hours and late that afternoon Bill's parents and each of his five siblings committed their lives to Christ."

This remarkable turn of events touched Cheryl in such a profound way that to recount it now, two decades later, brings her to tears. "When we heard about what happened, I started thinking much more deeply about what my salvation cost God the Father. Before, I don't think I really understood what it must have been like for the Father to sacrifice His Son. His sacrifice is all the more astounding by comparison because I didn't give my daughter willingly. If someone had said to me, 'Would you sacrifice your daughter so that Bill's family could come to know Christ?'" Her voice cracking, she whispers, "How could I do that? How could I have that much love? And yet that's how much love God the Father had for us, to give His Son's life—even while we were rejecting Him. Harder than giving our life is to give our child's life. I mean, what parent could give their child to save somebody else? But God did that for us."

As time passed, Cheryl heard more and more encouraging news about Bill's family—that Michael's aunts, uncles and cousins were getting involved in church life and that his grandfather was becoming a new man. Then one day, Cheryl saw it herself. "Bill's father was at the house to pick up Michael when he noticed a photo of Dawn. With his head bowed low, he said, 'I am so sorry for what my family has done to your family,' and he started crying. In that moment, I could see God was changing him—and me as well. All of the resentment I had toward him just melted away."

It's moments like this, Cheryl says, that point to God's intimate involvement in our lives. "I am learning that we are either aware of the presence of God in our lives or are totally oblivious. All the things that our family has walked through have opened my eyes to His constant work, and it's been like a protective shield for my heart—protecting me and our whole family from being defeated by evil. Life is such a miracle, such an amazing adventure. I have never thought that I am an especially brave person, but God has shown me that He can use every challenge and every trial to bring blessing if we trust Him with it. He's given us the grace to do that, and now all we can say is, 'Look what God has done!'"

# 5.

# I AM the Truth

"Four words. That's our goal for Immanuel," the medical director reminded his newest staff psychotherapist during their weekly case review. "If you can get Immanuel to speak four coherent words, we'll call that a success."

Dr. Richard Ganz opened Immanuel's file and reviewed the most salient points. *Vietnam war vet. Catatonic. Schizophrenic. No significant verbal communication for four years.* Internally, Rich groaned, feeling sorrow for this man's condition, and wondered if all his years of training to be a psychotherapist could really help this patient, or anyone for that matter.

It was a question that weighed heavily on his mind. A conversation he had had on a city bus with a colleague a while back flashed through his mind.

"All these techniques we are using are often ineffective and basically meaningless!" Rich confided to his friend.

"Look out that window and tell me what you see," Rich's colleague said.

"I see people digging ditches—in ninety-degree heat," Rich said.

"You had better be careful about what you say or you will be out there digging ditches with them."

It was hardly the insight Rich had been looking for.

It had only been a few years since that conversation, but during that time Dr. Ganz's priorities had changed so radically, it might as well have been a hundred. As he walked back to his office and took in the clinical surroundings, he contemplated the surprising course his life had taken. He had been raised in an Orthodox Jewish family in the South Bronx, the borough in New York City where, if you wanted the butcher down the block to save you something special, it wouldn't hurt to know a little Yiddish. Even as a child, he knew the proper way to tie the tefillin to his arm and head, according to God's commandment to the Israelites.[1] Every day, before *and* after school, he was in the synagogue, learning to recite countless passages of Scripture in Hebrew. And who could forget the way the adults spoke about their relatives lost in the Holocaust and the way they practically spat the words *Christian* and *Jesus Christ*?

---

1. And these words that I command you today shall be on your heart. You shall teach them diligently to your children, and shall talk of them when you sit in your house, and when you walk by the way, and when you lie down, and when you rise. You shall bind them as a sign on your hand, and they shall be as frontlets between your eyes (Deut. 6:6-8).

In a thousand ways, he was taught certain attitudes about Gentiles—and this about himself: *you are Jewish; stay away from the goyim. They hate us and want to kill us.*

But despite these things, he had made it; he was *a doctor of clinical psychology*, the apple of his mother's eye, the boy who won prizes for bringing friends to the synagogue, a boy from the South Bronx now headed to a practice at Upstate Medical Center, a prestigious medical center in upstate New York.

But by the time Rich was entering his new position, things with his mom couldn't have been worse. From Hannah Ganz's perspective, the diplomas on Rich's wall could in no way make up for the little New Testament he now carried around in his shirt pocket. Even spurning Judaism and turning atheist, as Rich had for a number of years, was better than Christianity. "Why?!" his mother cried, when he first told her about his conversion to Christianity. "How could this be?" she said, absolutely beside herself. "You were in synagogue every day. You made a pilgrimage to Israel! I cannot even process this! Do not even talk to me. Consider yourself dead!"

*Was this what was in store for him—being disowned by those whom he loved the most?* It grieved him terribly. And yet he understood her anger and animosity. Completely. All he had to do was recall how utterly torn into pieces he felt that day, several months prior, when he was confronted with the 53rd chapter of Isaiah, when everything he had formerly believed about Jesus came crashing down on his head.

It all started unremarkably enough—a vacation in Europe, a time for Rich and his wife Nancy to celebrate his job offer at the hospital. They had the whole thing mapped out. But day by day, through wild, unexpected twists and turns, they ended up in a village in Holland, being warmly welcomed at a place called L'Abri Fellowship—a house that seemed to operate a lot like a hostel, except room and board were free, and dinner was often followed by scholarly lectures by esteemed professors. A professor from M.I.T. set the stage their first night with a lecture entitled *Quantum Mechanics and its Relationship to God*. "I had no idea what he was talking about," Rich said. "One thing I learned from this lecture: At least some Christians were certainly not as stupid as I had thought they were."

Over the course of the week, Rich and Nancy learned that philosophical and religious insights were standard fare in virtually every discussion at L'Abri. "They were incredibly interesting," Rich said. "As a man with no sense of God, I saw myself as nothing better than a chance accumulation of molecules in an absurd and meaningless world. I listened and talked to these people, questioning and mocking their beliefs." Then, one day, the leader at L'Abri, a man named Hans Van Seventer, asked Rich if he could read to him "something from the Bible."

Wary, but willing, Rich consented.

Hans flipped open the Bible and started reading:

See, my Servant will act wisely; he will be raised and lifted up and highly exalted. Just as there were many who were appalled at him – his appearance was so disfigured beyond that of any man and his form marred beyond human likeness – so will he sprinkle many nations, and kings will shut their mouths because of him. For what they were not told, they will see, and what they have not heard, they will understand.[2]

Who has believed our message and to whom has the arm of the Lord been revealed? He grew up before him like a tender shoot, and like a root out of dry ground. He had no beauty or majesty to attract us to him, nothing in his appearance that we should desire him. He was despised and rejected by men, a man of sorrows and familiar with suffering. Like one from whom men hide their faces he was despised, and we esteemed him not.[3]

*I've heard that expression before,* Rich thought—*"a man of sorrows and familiar with suffering." But where?* Then suddenly Rich understood—Hans was reading to him about Jesus. *Does he know what he is doing, reading this Christian stuff to a Jew?* Rich told himself to be patient as Hans continued.

Surely He has borne our griefs and carried our sorrows; yet we considered him stricken, smitten by God, and afflicted. He was pierced for our transgressions.

---

2. Isaiah 52:13-15 (NIV)

3. The remaining verses in this section are all from Isaiah 53 (NIV)

Images of Renaissance paintings leapt to Rich's mind, paintings with Jesus hanging on a cross, pierced. *What is Hans' agenda here?* Rich asked himself, the anger rising in him.

> He was crushed for our iniquities. The punishment that brought us peace was upon him, and by his wounds we are healed. We all like sheep have gone astray; each of us has turned to his own way; and the LORD has laid on him the iniquity of us all.

Bristling with indignation, Rich could barely contain himself. *This was nothing less than an anti-Semitic assault. But he knew how he would counter. In a moment, he would blast Hans: This easy way out of your guilt—it's irresponsible! All you have to say is Jesus took away your sins! How convenient—you found a cheap way out of long-term psychoanalysis.*

Hans could not know he was unlocking vaults of old memories, frightening memories Rich had from when he was seven and, in an act of daring, snuck into a Catholic church. Looming from on high were images and impressions that seared powerfully into his brain. Jesus was Catholic, *obviously.* And—judging by his tall, delicate, slightly anorexic frame, his long silken blond hair and piercing blue eyes—*Scandinavian.*

"I had gotten as far as the vestibule of that Catholic church, when I looked at one of the statues and thought that the ground was going to open and swallow me up. I thought that I was damned forever just for looking at that statue. I ran eight blocks home to get away from what I considered to be an unpardonable sin. But these 'Catholics' had it all worked out. No long-term therapy. Jesus pays and they go free. What a deal!"

If Hans picked up on Rich's discomfort, he didn't comment, but instead read on.

He was oppressed and afflicted, yet he did not open his mouth. He was led like a lamb to the slaughter, and as a sheep before its shearers is silent, so he did not open his mouth. By oppression and judgment, he was taken away; and who can speak of his descendants? For he was cut off from the land of the living; for the transgression of my people he was stricken. He was assigned a grave with the wicked, but with the rich in his death...

In Rich's mind, he saw paintings of Jesus on the cross, and the two thieves, one on either side of Him. *I've seen these things in museums,* Rich thought with growing irritation. *He's not telling me anything new.*

...though he had done no violence, nor was any deceit in his mouth. Yet it was the Lord's will to crush him and cause him to suffer. Though the Lord makes his life a guilt offering, he will see his offspring and prolong his days, and the will of the Lord will prosper in his hand.

Rich rolled his eyes. *This whole scene is absurd. These people never stop. Here they go with that myth about the resurrection. Why can't they accept the fact that once a person is*

*dead, he is dead? Grow up! Put away your infantile neuroses*
*and realize that when you are dead, you are dead. That is it.*

> He will see the light of life and be satisfied. By his
> knowledge my righteous servant will justify many, and
> he will bear their iniquities. Therefore I will give him a
> portion among the great, and he will divide the spoils
> with the strong, because he poured out his life unto
> death, and was numbered with the transgressors. For
> he bore the sin of many, and made intercession for the
> transgressors.

At last, Hans finished reading. He looked at Rich
and said, "What do you think?"

By this time, Rich was brimming with choice
retorts, absolutely convinced Hans had just read
a passage from his Gentile Bible, and that it
was a report of someone who had witnessed the
crucifixion.

Rich responded without a moment's hesitation:
"Anyone who was there at that cross could have
written that stuff! What does that prove?"

Hans handed Rich the Bible. "In that millisecond,"
Rich recalls, "my life was shattered. The name that
I saw at the top of the page was *Isaiah*! Hans had
been reading to me from *MY* Bible, from *my Hebrew
Scriptures*, and I felt as though someone had taken a
sword and cut me to pieces."

Rich sat dumbfounded, his eyes transfixed on
that name, Isaiah.

"Rich," Hans said, "Isaiah was written 700 years before Jesus was born."

"I felt as if I had been stabbed to death," Rich said. "It hit me like an explosive, it was so beyond my ability to assimilate. I felt myself moaning. I was sitting there practically going crazy. Because I knew it was true. I knew it right then and there. As much as I couldn't stand it, I believed it. And I thought, I'm being torn to pieces. This is the roughest experience of my life! Why couldn't it be anyone else? Why couldn't it be Krishna? Why couldn't it be Buddha? Why does it have to be *Him?*

"Prior to that day, the one thing I had going for me as an unbeliever was that I was always looking for truth. The moment I saw Isaiah printed at the top of that page, I knew instantly, Jesus was Truth. Though I didn't have the knowledge or the words to express this at the time, I knew beyond a shadow of a doubt that the One who is the Truth was in that room and He was speaking to me.

"That's the power of the word of God. The word of God brought the truth claims of Christ to complete fruition in my life instantaneously. I knew immediately that if Jesus wrote history about Himself in my Bible, that if the Gentile God was the Jewish God and He was truly God, then I had to submit everything to Him for the rest of my life. It was with this conviction that I left L'Abri."

Rich returned to the U.S. terrified at what his conversion might mean for him, but hopeful for his relatives. Was it unrealistic, he wondered, to think the word of God would have the same powerful impact on them? When they heard Isaiah 53, surely they'd be instantly convinced as well. But this wasn't the case. His mother's antagonism turned out to be just a foretaste of the rejection and hostility he'd receive from his brother, cousins, aunts and uncles, all of whom refused to speak to him or have anything to do with him after he told them about Yeshua. His mother even removed him from her will.

"At first, their reaction surprised me," Rich said, "but then I saw that unbelief was part of the prophesy too. 'Who has believed our message? ... he was despised and rejected by men ... and we esteemed him not.'"[4]

"Somebody later asked me how I dealt with losing all those relationships," Rich said. "I was really sad—but not for myself. I didn't want to lose my mom to hell. Telling my family about Christ cost me a lot, but by that point I was determined to not focus on myself. When I was in training to be a psychotherapist, I was required to undergo psychotherapy and I went for psychoanalysis three times a week. It was all about me. And it was pointless. But when I became a Christian, I knew— this can't be about me anymore. From that moment on, I didn't have the energy or time or interest to

---

4. Isaiah 53:1-2 (NIV)

focus on myself. My life was devoted to telling anyone and everyone the truth about Yeshua."[5]

It was a mercy that Rich had only the vaguest notion of the tremendous conflict his commitment to Jesus would bring.

One day, not long after starting his new position, Rich was astonished to get a call from his brother Neal. "I thought you disowned me," Rich said.

"I'm just relaying a message, Rich," he said, flatly. "Mom is in the hospital. She wants you to come see her."

"The hospital! Why? What's happening?"

"She needed a skin graft—because of her cancer. She shouldn't be there long, but she wants you to come see her."

Marking his calendar to take two days off work later that Friday, Rich shook his head in wonder. The last time he had been with his mom, things were bleak. Even though she was on her own— Rich's father had died when he was twelve—and was recovering from cancer, she didn't want to see or hear from Rich, especially if he was going to say another word about Jesus. When Rich called, before she could hang up, Rich would say, "Mom, I just want to pray for you." Or "Mom, I just want to read to you from the book of Job." She would listen for a bit, but that was the extent of their interactions. *What's so serious it requires seeing me in person? I guess I'll find out on Friday.*

---

5. Yeshua is the Hebrew way to say Jesus.

But before that Friday came, Neal called with terrible news: their mom had died unexpectedly from an aneurism.

Rich pressed the receiver against his forehead, stunned into silence. As the first waves of shock and grief washed over him, Neal blasted him with an angry accusation: "Rich, I better not find out what you did to Mom!" he yelled.

"What? I don't know what you're talking about. I didn't do anything to Mom."

"How dare you tell Mom she was dying a Christian?"

"I didn't say that to her."

"Yes, you did! You told her she's dying a Christian! What did you *do* to her?"

"I have no idea. I didn't even speak with her. Back off, man. Lay off of me."

On the drive to New York, and throughout the funeral, he ruminated. *Where would Neal have heard she's dying a Christian? What could that mean? What is this all about?* Then he remembered she'd been in the hospital for a number of days. As the service ended, Rich turned to Nancy and said, "We've got to get to the hospital. We've got to find the people who were with Mom and find out what happened."

It didn't take long for Rich and Nancy to find the three women who shared a hospital room with his mom. They willingly gave him the full report of her last days:

"We thought your mom was crazy."

"Yeah, she was pacing around the room yelling curses at Jesus Christ for what he did to you."

"We'd never seen anything like it. It was bizarre."

"We decided to call our churches. The three of us are Christians. We asked our churches to line up people to pray for her for twenty-four straight hours."

"We asked her, 'How did you come to hate Jesus?' She said, 'My son, my son. He's into this Jesus thing.'"

"One morning she came up to us. She said, 'Why is it ... You women are dying. I know that. You know that. I'm just here for a skin graft—it's nothing—but I'm going crazy and you're at peace. What is it you ladies have that I need to know about?'"

"We told her, 'What you need to know about is not what you want to hear. What you need to know about is the person you've been cursing: Jesus.'"

The rest of the day turned into an intense Q and A session.

"I've heard this *over and over* from my son," Hannah said. "I've rejected my son. I've taken him out of my will. I'll have to change that. I didn't want to see him or talk to him because of this Jesus. Now here I am saying I believe in Him. I believe in a Savior who paid for my sins, who also faced a tortuous death. So what happens now?"

"We told her to have the chaplain come explain about being baptized. Together, they made a plan to do that after you arrived."

"But the next day was when she had that burst aneurism. The chaplain was in. She was covered with blood. He said, 'Hannah. We need to do the baptism now.' She was baptized and passed away."

"She said to us, 'I'm dying a Christian.'"

Rich and Nancy expressed their heart-felt gratitude to the ladies, and walked out of the hospital in a state of awe. "My brother got it right," Rich said. "She died a Christian. But it wasn't me. It was the ladies at the hospital and the chaplain."

They decided the next stop needed to be at Neal's apartment. "I started to talk to him about Yeshua," Rich said, "and I handed him a huge study Bible. He grabbed it and hurled it at my head, shouting, 'It's time for you to get out of here!' It whizzed by me, missing me by barely an inch. In my mind's eye, I saw my obituary: *Dr. Richard Ganz killed by the Word of God*."

On their way back upstate, Rich thought about his mom—now in the presence of Jesus. He breathed a sigh of relief. It could so easily have gone the other way. The last time they spoke, Hannah *hated* Jesus. How thankful he was that he did not shrink back from saying what needed to be said, even though it meant a dark cloud of antagonism hung over their last months together. *I never got to spend a moment with her as a believer. It cost me, being the one to challenge her beliefs. But one day I will see her again.* He tried to imagine what that reunion would be like—but who can think about such things while you're driving? His brother still hated him with a white-hot passion. *But he now has a Bible.*

More than ever, he was grateful for Nancy. What a blessing that she too came to faith in Christ at L'Abri Fellowship. Together, they would pray for Neal and the other relatives. Together they would figure out what it meant to live for Christ.

That was a big question, especially for Rich in his work at the psychiatric hospital. He knew from all the years he spent earning his doctorate that the world of academics and medicine largely viewed Christians with ridicule, if not outright contempt. It felt crazy to think about how hard he had worked to prepare for that job, only to feel now like a fish out of water.

But he reminded himself to be encouraged by his experience with his mom. Lately he had been weaving scripture into his conversations with his patients. Yes, biblical communication with the patients was understood to be taboo, but his patients were responding so favorably—everyday he saw marked improvements—it was hard to imagine that the administration would take a hardline approach.

Rich didn't realize his colleagues had also noticed the results he was getting, till one day he was given a new case—a 350-pound man who came barreling at top speed into the elevator and careened into Rich, nearly crushing his 165-pound frame against the back wall.

"Listen," Rich asked a couple of his colleagues that day who were responsible for giving the patient assignments, "why do you keep giving me the most psychotic cases?"

"Because they were hopeless," one of them said. "And you're doing something for them."

"Right," said the other. "We don't know what you're doing, but whatever it is, it's working."

"Well, one thing," Rich said, "is to not consider anyone hopeless."

Then one day Rich inadvertently walked into another psychotherapist's office while he was in the middle of a session. He was sitting on the floor in the lotus position, wearing Buddhist garb, reciting a mantra, doing what Rich could only guess was Buddhist therapy.

"I asked him about it," Rich said, "and suggested he come observe what I was doing. I figured, if he can get away with Buddhist stuff, I wouldn't get in trouble for what I was doing. Unlike him," he said, laughing, "I didn't even need a uniform."

But the problem wasn't with the garb.

"Look," his colleague said, after observing Rich, "they don't mind what I'm doing. But *you*—you aren't long for this place."

"*Why?*" Rich asked. "*You're* long for this place."

"They don't mind what I'm doing," he said again. "But they'll mind what *you're* doing. I'm telling you, you better stop."

"I can't stop."

"Why not?"

"Because it's the right thing to do."

He felt the rightness of it deep within. "These people were desperate," Rich said, "and I knew from my experience at my conversion that there is enormous power in the Word of God. It truly is sharper than a double-edged sword, cutting to the deepest part of your being.[6] And I was immersing myself in the Scriptures, so I was coming to know Him as a Rock, steadfast, the God of armies with strength and power that He uses for us. Not some wimpy little god, but the God of heaven and earth—someone you can trust. I was reading *and seeing* that He will never leave you or forsake you. He will take care of you. I could see that everything in the Scriptures points to a God who is trustworthy. As I went through my day, I was always looking for an opportunity to share these truths."

Sometimes, opportunities rolled out before Rich like a red carpet—as when Immanuel's behavior drew everyone's attention in a group therapy session one morning. As the patients were gathering, Immanuel suddenly started to take in deep, anxious breaths. In a matter of moments, he was hyperventilating. Then, as all eyes looked on in shock, his body started to spasm violently and writhe in agony. "What is it, Immanuel?" Rich cried, "Get it out!"

"I am Jesus Christ!" Immanuel screamed.

---

6. See Hebrews 4:12

Rich whipped out the small New Testament from his pocket. Just that morning he had read Matthew 24. He quoted it to him. "Then if anyone says to you, 'Behold, here is the Christ,' or 'There He is,' do not believe him. For false christs and false prophets will arise and will show great signs and wonders, so as to mislead, if possible, even the elect. ... For just as the lightning comes from the east and flashes even to the west, so shall the coming of the Son of Man be."

No sooner were those words spoken than Immanuel stood stock still, his writhing gone, his breathing normalized. Calmly, he asked, "Where is that from?"

*Four words,* Rich thought—*four coherent words—from Immanuel, whom no one could get to say a word!* Shaking off his astonishment, Rich tossed him the Bible, saying, "It's all in here. Read it. That's where you're going to get the answers you need, right there."

Over the next four weeks, Immanuel did not say another word. Rich, busy with his case load, almost forgot about that interaction—until one day while eating lunch at his desk, Immanuel showed up— speaking again—this time with words that would mark the beginning of the end of Rich's career as a clinical psychologist.

"I want to become a Christian," Immanuel said.

Rich swallowed hard. "For the past eight months I'd been praying fervently for an opportunity to lead someone to faith in Christ. I thought it'd be at a Bible study or with a family member, I never thought it'd be at the hospital."

Somehow, this seemed beyond all of his other spiritually-oriented conversations. This was conversion. *Conversion!* Rich knew he was facing the point of no return. In his head, conflicting desires vied for dominance.

*Immanuel wants to become a Christian! This is amazing and wonderful!*

*But if I do this, I could lose everything I've worked for. And I don't know how to do anything else!*

*Everything you've been telling your family about Yeshua— Do you believe it?*

*Yes, absolutely. All of it!*

*I'm such a lousy coward. If I lose my job, how am I going to support myself?*

*Does God know how to take care of you? Isn't this in Immanuel's best interests?*

*Yes, He does. And yes, it is.*

The matter was settled. In that next hour, Rich's office became a place of new birth. Rising from his knees, Immanuel grasped Rich's hand with both hands and pumped his arm, eyes bright and smile radiant. Rich felt a warmth flood over him. What a gift—to be a part of this man's startling—no— miraculous transformation! With a mixed sense of foreboding and excitement, Rich trembled a little, knowing this day would, sooner or later, impact his future.

Not even twenty-four hours later Rich got called into the medical director's office.

"Rich, I've just heard the craziest story," Dr. Elias Applebaum[7] said. "You won't believe it."

"Oh, a crazy story. I'd love to hear it," Rich said. "Tell me."

"I've heard Immanuel is going around telling people he is saved and that you're responsible for this."

"No, Elias. He's got one thing wrong. Yes, he is saved, but God alone is responsible for saving someone's soul. I can't do anything about that. He has come to faith in Christ and he's simply trying to say I was involved."

"Oh, no! You're a Jewish Jesus freak!"

"I'm not a freak. But you've got the other parts of it right. Look, Elias. How many words did Immanuel use? You told me I'd be a great success if we could get him to speak four words coherently. Here's a guy who was in a catatonic state. He couldn't speak, he couldn't move, he couldn't do anything. He's speaking coherently now. Nobody is even saying to me, "Wonderful work, good job!"

"We don't want him talking about this Jesus. This is not psychotherapy. Look what you've done to the guy. Before he couldn't speak, but listen to what he's talking about. He's talking nonsense about Jesus Christ. He's telling all the patients and staff on the ward that he's repented of all of his sins and Jesus is his Savior. He sounds like you. Here's what he said to me. He said Jesus Christ saved him

---

7. A pseudonym

and he's going to live forever. I said, 'Where did you get this from?' He said, 'Oh, Dr. Ganz told me everything I know. He knows all about Jesus. If you have any questions, just ask him. He'll answer all your questions.'"

"I don't know everything."

"Look, here's what's involved, Rich. There were 212 applicants for your job. You got it. You went from your post doctorate studies right into a position where you are on the faculty of the medical center. You're teaching graduate classes at the university. You have your own private practice. Why are you messing this up? Look, I don't care if you do this outside of work. I just want you to promise me that you'll never do this again on the job because I don't want you to leave here."

*Oh, my goodness,* Rich thought. *He's asking me to deny Christ.*

"We'll take care of Immanuel," Elias said. "We'll just send him to another hospital and do a series of ECT treatments.[8] He won't even remember what this is all about. He'll forget the whole thing."

"Elias," Rich said, "Before long you'll be sending *me* to get those shock treatments. But you know we can't do that to Immanuel. That would be horrible. That is evil. That is wrong. We aren't going to do that. Don't try to get Immanuel to forget—this is the one thing that's going to give him a good life. But give me twenty-four hours to consider your

---

8. Electroconvulsive therapy (ECT) is a procedure that sends small electric currents through the brain. It often erases memories.

offer about not bringing Jesus into my work with my patients."

As he headed home that day, Rich's mind reeled with questions. *Should I accept what my authorities say? I've only been a Christian eight months. I really don't want to leave this, but I don't want to agree to those terms if that's wrong in God's eyes. Is there anything I can read? Is there any book that has been written on anything like this? Yes! The Book of Acts.*

That night Rich plowed through Acts two or three times. The next morning, he came straight to the point in Elias's office. "The book of Acts teaches that I must obey God rather than men.[9] What my eyes have seen, and my ears have heard, these things I must speak. Thank you for offering me something like that, but I cannot accept your condition. I have to tell what I know to be true."

"Well, Rich, I'm sorry," Elias said, "but we cannot have that here. We'll give you thirty days to tie up loose ends before your work is finished here."

Once again, Rich's thoughts went back to all the time and money he had spent on his education. *This is what I have spent all my life preparing to do. And now it's over. I have no savings and I have no clue what I'm going to do now. I have no other skill sets. I haven't trained to be a mechanic or anything else. Can I even get a recommendation from anyone here? My colleagues will think of me as some psychotic who just blew up his career. I'll be blacklisted, and they'll be afraid to associate with me. This is the hardest time of my life.*

---

9. Acts 5:29

But even while these thoughts circled around in his brain, he felt a stabilizing presence. "I knew God was going to take care of me. I just knew that must mean that God had something better planned for me." The specifics?—unclear. But one thing was obvious: Rich's life would center around making the truth of the Gospel known to the people in his path.

Shortly after that, two of his colleagues came to him at night, secretly gave him a glowing reference, and said, "We love what you do, but we came here tonight because we do not want to risk our colleagues seeing us with you."

The day after his conversation with Elias, Rich awoke with a sense of urgency about his thirty remaining days. *One month!* he thought as a hundred faces, staff and patients, raced through his mind. So, on the day he encountered Stanley Goldstein, curled up, as usual, on the floor in a fetal position, Rich was on fire.

"Stanley, you've had all the therapies and drug therapies. Nothing at all has helped you. Will you let me help you?" Stanley just remained curled up in silence. Taking a deep breath, Rich shouted, "Stanley Goldstein, in the name of Jesus Christ, stand up!"

Immediately, Stanley jumped to his feet, enraged, and shouted in Rich's face, "I'm an Orthodox Jew! How dare you speak to me about Jesus!?"

"You'd *better* listen!" Rich said. "You're on the floor useless and hopeless. You *need* Jesus. He is the promised Messiah of the Jewish people."

Stanley's eyes blazed with fury. "I'm going to prove you're wrong!"

And with that, he spun on his heels and stomped off down the hall, telling him that he was going to the nearby bookstore to buy a Bible and prove him wrong.

Rich watched Stanley blow past a startled nurse, wondering how he managed to alienate so many people for whom he cared so deeply. But he knew the answer full well: it was the truth that did it. He considered all the conflict that Jesus—the Person of Truth—encountered in His relationships. He remembered, too, how the apostles were flogged for speaking the truth and yet "left the Sanhedrin rejoicing because they had been counted worthy of suffering disgrace for the Name."[10]

If he was going to follow in Christ's steps, how could he *even hope* for all his interactions to be pleasant? The revelation was freeing. *The truth will set you free,*[11] he recalled. Again, the uncertainty of his future came to mind, but this time without fear or regret. *I have no idea what I'm going to do, but if this is what a surrendered life looks like—all this warfare—so be it. I'm not looking for a life of niceness, or something peaceful or sweet or soft.*

The question was, how would joblessness affect these convictions? Even more so, how would enticing job *offers?* Given the circumstances surrounding his departure, Rich was amazed when a Christian

---

10. Acts 5:41 (NIV)
11. John 8:32

psychiatrist in New York City asked him to come be his partner, offering him a luxurious office on Madison Avenue. In addition to seeing patients, the job also entailed co-hosting a radio program for one of the biggest markets in the country. The prestige, the lifestyle, the fame—it could have been his for the taking. But Rich asked to have one year to pray about the offer, and it was granted.

During that year, Rich realized that his only recourse, if he was going to do the work he felt certain God was calling him to do, was to go back to square one and enter seminary. To start all over again, *a freshman in his late twenties*, felt tremendously humbling. Under the mentorship of Dr. Jay Adams[12] at Westminster Theological Seminary, Rich learned the ropes of Biblical counseling, earning a whopping $5/hour. "We rented a very old farm house outside of Philadelphia and lived on bushels of tomatoes and corn we bought from a farmer for a few dollars. It didn't matter because all I wanted was to study theology and immerse myself in the Scriptures."

"Dr. Adams used to tell me when I asked to have a job in his counseling center, 'I don't care how many degrees you have. If you want to say, "Thus sayeth the Lord," you'd better know what the Lord says!'" There's no way Dr. Adams could have known what an impact those words would have on the rest of Rich's life. All that would follow—from

---

12. The renowned Dr. Jay Adams is the father of the biblical counseling movement and the author of over 100 books on the subject.

becoming a Biblical counselor, evangelist, and best-selling author,[13] to pastoring a church in Ottawa, Canada—would center around knowing what the Lord said and speaking that truth to anyone who crossed his path: gas station attendants, waitresses, fellow diners and theater-goers, fellow kick-boxing enthusiasts, and—out of a deep yearning and affection for his people—unbelieving Jews.

But it's not like he had to barge down doors for a hearing. Not at all. Like the time Rich decided to take Nancy to an Orthodox synagogue on the eve of Yom Kippur. "I was a believer for a year and I wanted Nancy to see what the High Holidays were all about. As soon as we entered the synagogue, it was like I was being brought back twelve years. As a youth, I didn't have any connection to God, but now I did. And the opportunity to worship there, to sing those same songs and hear those same passages ... I was overcome with the joy of knowing my life is hidden with Christ in God.[14] I was rejoicing and weeping when suddenly the rabbi stopped the service. I didn't know why and looked around, wondering what was happening."

"The rabbi called out, 'We have here a young Judean who is rejoicing in the Lord.' I was looking around me and he said, 'No, don't look around. It's *you*. I want you now to share with us how you are

---

13.*Psychobabble: The Failure of Modern Psychology—and the Biblical Alternative* is one of seven books authored by Dr. Ganz. It has been endorsed by Dr. John MacArthur and Dr. J. I. Packer.

14.Colossians 3:3

rejoicing in the Lord with tears and joy and singing. How did this happen to you? Tell us, please.'"

"I immediately shared my testimony, but in the midst of it they stopped me. The rabbi went ballistic. He said, 'The service is over! Everyone is leaving the synagogue. Right now. Everyone is to go immediately from this place. We have a *meshumad*, an apostate, here.'"

The synagogue was packed; hundreds were there for the service.

"Go home," the rabbi continued, shouting, "and remember a Jew gets to heaven by following one law every day! Here's the law for today: Stay away from the *meshumad*, if you want to go to heaven."

"I can't believe this," Rich said, mostly to Nancy. "People are going to go to heaven if they don't talk to me. That's quite impressive, isn't it?"

"Rich," Nancy said, "this is not a joke."

Outside, Rich and Nancy decided to lay hands on the synagogue and pray out loud for the people. In a matter of minutes, they were surrounded by two dozen young people from inside.

"We're very interested in what the rabbi said, and what you said in there. We want you to tell us more about this."

"I'd be glad to," Rich said. Finding a place nearby to sit, Rich began telling them about the joy of knowing Yeshua. "They had never had that kind of experience and were asking questions when all of a sudden three really big freaky-looking guys marched up to the group."

"All of you—out of here, now!" they roared, waving their arms menacingly and jabbing the air with staccato fingers.

"Excuse me," Rich interjected, "I don't think they want to leave here now."

"You didn't hear us, did you? Do you know who we are?"

"I think I'm getting an idea. You're in the Jewish Defense League, here to protect our people from me."

"Yes, you got it right, and if you don't shut up you're going to need someone to not only protect you, but to pick you off the ground if you're still alive. So you better shut up."

"Wait a second. Why don't you three stay here and hang out with me and my wife. We can talk together for a while, okay? What do you think about that?"

"We think you're a lunatic. So just stop it. Don't talk to us. And these young people are not going to be here. They're gone. Do you understand?"

"They don't want to go."

"It doesn't matter. It doesn't matter to *us*. Our job is to keep our people away from people like *you!*"

"But didn't you see? I know all the songs. I can sing them in Hebrew. I was rejoicing—the only one in the synagogue who was rejoicing. That's why the rabbi asked. Don't you get it? The rabbi was interested. So let's pretend the rabbi is here. We'll talk about why I rejoice like that."

"You are trying our patience. *We're* not staying here with you and *they* are not staying here with you. Just shut up and let everyone go."

There was nothing left to be said—at least at that moment. Tomorrow was another day—Yom Kippur—and Rich, his veins coursing with holy adrenaline, was already thinking ahead.

Nancy could hardly believe her ears. "You really want to go back there?" she said the next morning. "They want to *kill* you. They don't think you're funny or interesting or more spiritual. They find you to be *horrible*. They want to take your life. That's what they do, to protect Jews from Jews like you now. You really want to go back?"

"Of course I'm going. I'd love to have you come with me. I guarantee they won't touch you. They won't even have to know you're with me. Let's just go. I'll keep a low profile. I think we're meant to be there. We have some kind of ministry."

"You know what those guys said. They think you're doing this on purpose. They're going to bust out of the woodwork to do something right in the sanctuary."

Nancy was partially right. As soon as the rabbi laid eyes on Rich, he startled everyone with this abrupt announcement: "Here's what happens today," he said, abandoning the customary order of prayers. "I want every single male to come up. I'm going to give a blessing to every male."

The implication wasn't lost on Rich: The blessing was intended to be a shield of protection against him and his influence. Forgetting his promise to be low-profile, Rich called out, "Why not every woman too?" The rabbi would get his revenge for that. Later. After the service, when Rich and Nancy were making their way home, a group of large, young men rushed up and planted themselves inches in front of them.

"Hi guys, how are you doing?" Rich asked, hoping friendly nonchalance would defuse their aggression.

"We're not here to talk," one of them snarled.

"I didn't come to you. You came to me. So why are you here?"

"Because we have something for you to *do*! You're a really religious guy, *right*? We want *you* to get down on your *face* on the *floor* and *pray for us* if you're so [expletive] religious!"

*Oh, this is not going to be fun,* Rich thought, but found himself saying, "Okay, it would be my pleasure," and got down on the ground and began to pray out loud, waiting for a boot to come crashing down on his neck. But it never came.

"Enough, *enough* praying for us," they shouted. "Get up, *get up*! Stop!"

"I wasn't done."

"I *know* you weren't done. You're *never* going to be done," one of them shouted, waving his arms like an umpire calling an out. "The day's over. You're done. Done! Stop, stop, stop!"

"I'm not doing anything. You are the ones doing things. Why can't you see I'm just a nice Jewish boy from the Bronx?"

This seemed to stop them in their tracks. "You're from the *Bronx*? Where did you ever get this Jesus stuff?"

"That's a good question. Let me tell you."

"No, we don't want to know how you became a *meshumad*. We don't want to know that."

"Yes, yes you do. You are interested. You are wondering. Look, I was more religious than you've ever been. I was *davening*[15] every morning and every evening in the synagogue. I was thirteen years old and the next closest to me in age was seventy."

They seemed to bounce between hatred and curiosity. "Oh, you know Hebrew?"

"Yes, of course I know Hebrew. I went to the synagogue every morning and evening as I just said. I put on the tefillin before the service in the morning. I prayed with the tallit[16], a beautiful one given to me on my bar mitzvah. You know, I'm a Jew of Jews. You're not going to find someone more Jewish than me."

"Then how could you have done this?"

"That's what I want to explain to you."

---

15.Davening is praying in the synagogue worship.

16.A Jewish prayer shawl

"No, no. We've got to get out of here," one of them said, anxiously. "Let's get out of here before he proves it to us. We'll never meet again, I'm hoping. Goodbye."

Marveling at their speed, their evident fear of hearing something convincing, Rich chuckled, mentally putting words to the pattern that so often described his life: *I care. I speak the truth. They run away.*

But not everyone runs. Some *initiate* spiritual conversations and ask probing questions. Rich's Muslim physician, for example, paused mid-way through Rich's appointment one day to say, "I am a thoroughly devout Muslim. My life is given over to Allah. Tell me what will happen to me when I die." Rich gave him the straight scoop, saying "Without Christ you will go to hell."

"He came over and hugged me, and said, 'Thank you! You are the first Christian to tell me the truth. I have asked approximately 200 Christians during my life this question. These were men who assured me they were believing Christians. I know what the Bible says in answer to my question. You are the first person who ever told me the truth. Now I know that I can ask you any question I want, because this is the most difficult question and you didn't waver even for a second. You immediately told me the truth. I know that I can ask you anything and you will always tell me the truth.' Now, whenever I have an appointment, he tells his staff to clear his afternoon so he has time to ask me all his questions."

Other times, run-aways come back. Like when Rich's brother Neal called six months after their mother's funeral. In their first interaction since the Bible-as-projectile-incident, Neal asked to come see Rich—and upon arriving announced he was ready to become a Christian. In the years that followed, Rich watched Neal parlay their mother's inheritance into a multi-million-dollar business, and then sell it to run a ministry in Mexico for drug addicts and former prison inmates.

Likewise with Stanley Goldstein. The day he abandoned his fetal position, Stanley found a Bible and channeled his anger into studying the claims of Christ. In the few short weeks Rich had left working at the medical center, Stanley had come to believe—and was so transformed he was ready to be released from the hospital.

The same was true of Immanuel; no one who hears him speaking to groups of people today would ever imagine he had been mute for four years. "I remember the day I received a phone call," Rich said. "It was June 23, 2008. The caller said, 'Do you remember what happened on this day thirty-five years ago?'

I replied "Oh my, Immanuel."

"You remember me and that day?" he said.

"Immanuel, I'll never forget."

"Almost every year since," Rich said, "we continue to remember the goodness and mercy of God, how he had narrowly escaped the mind-ravaging effects of ECT treatments and had gone on to earn a college degree, marry, start a family, become an overseas missionary, and is now a grandfather."

"The three of us left the hospital on the same day," Rich remembers. "That day I was fired I thought it was the worst day of my life. Now, praise God, I know it was the best thing that ever happened to me.

"Being fired is what *needed* to happen," Rich said. "Now I can go around the country and the world telling people this: "When the Bible is open to you, and you come to hear and realize that Jesus truly is the way, and the truth, and the life, and that no one comes to the Father except through Jesus,[17] do you know what happens? I'll tell you what. Your life is now changed forever. Hang on! It is not going to be a smooth, soft, safe ride. It is going to be the ride of your life."

---

18. John 14:6

# 6.

# I AM Trustworthy

They had been spoiled. That's what Courtney and Grant decided—spoiled by the fact that their second son Ryan had been such a good-natured and compliant child—the easiest of their three by far.[1] Throughout his school years, Ryan was a diligent student with lots of diverse interests—football, electronics, model rockets—you name it. Granted, when the family moved from Iowa to Michigan in middle school, the adjustment was hard, especially for a quiet young man, but he eventually found friends—a good group of guys from the church youth group. *So far, so good*, his parents thought. Even in high school, the inevitable conflicts over their restrictions and direction were always resolved peaceably.

"This isn't bad," his father said. "We're still friends."

Before they knew it, Ryan was packing up for the University of Michigan. *All systems are go*, they

---

1. Some names and identifying details have been changed.

thought, fully expecting that in four years he'd emerge with his degree, not in some questionable major but in *engineering*—something marketable, in demand and secure. It was what they had worked and prayed so hard for. The day they moved Ryan into his freshman dorm, they were confident and happy. God had been very good to them. Things were going exactly according to plan.

They were happy, but honestly, in their hearts, not terribly surprised. After all, they had done things by the book—the Good Book. Didn't it follow that their three children would naturally grow up to love the Lord and contribute to society? It did. They *hoped* it did anyway. Their assurance wavered a little every time they saw other families struggling with wayward children. As an elder of a large church in Grand Rapids, Grant had seen it all and, along with Courtney, counseled dozens of parents through heartache and pain. It was a fearful thing to behold. *Could one of our kids do that?* they'd often wonder. *Don't they say children of church leaders are more targeted and more vulnerable than anyone? No,* they'd reassure themselves. *We're pouring our hearts out making sure that doesn't happen.*

How foolish that confidence seemed right now. Foolish and prideful, they fully admitted. There was simply no way of escaping the truth: Those easy years with Ryan had been a gift—a pure gift of grace, not a result of their fine parenting skills or anything else they thought they did right.

That's what years of anxiety would do—bring you to your knees in utter humility. Since the fall of Ryan's sophomore year, they had been in a battle, fighting *for* and fighting *with* Ryan about—who would have guessed?—his drinking. But they were losing—losing their rapport with Ryan, losing peace, losing their dreams for him to have a normal, productive life, and most of all, losing hope that they could do *anything* to get him off the fast-track to self-destruction. And tonight, like so many other nights before, they were losing any hope of sleep.

But this time was different—and scarier. Courtney and Grant had gotten used to Ryan calling at two in the morning. When the phone rang, their hearts would sink, knowing he was drunk again and that the call would consist mainly of rambling, sobbing, broken apologies. It tore their hearts out every time—or at least for the first half-dozen times—after which they weren't sure if they had anything left in their chest cavities.

But tonight, Ryan was clearly experiencing some kind of drunken delusion. Though they couldn't understand everything he said, it sounded like Ryan believed he had been poisoned. He had never acted so paranoid or talked such nonsense before. And what was he saying about drinking bleach? He was so incoherent, Courtney wasn't sure if he had already consumed bleach or if he just wanted to.

In tears, they raced over to his apartment. Finding the door ajar, they pushed it open to find

Ryan crawling around his living room floor amidst a small mountain of sofa cushions, dirty laundry and beer bottles. "I can't find my keys," Ryan cried. "I need to get some bleach and I can't find my keys!"

Hearing these words, Courtney and Grant exhaled, feeling the tension flow from their bodies. They soon understood everything: Someone in the bar had a malicious sense of humor—and a deranged imagination. The tale was that his drink had been spiked with a substance infected with AIDS. The "cure" was drinking bleach. *What kind of disturbed person would say that?* they wondered. *That is truly sick!* Courtney turned toward Grant and grasped his hands. Foreheads together, they whispered simple words of comfort: "He's okay. He's just drunk. He'll be fine in the morning."

Back at home, with Ryan sleeping it off in his old room, Courtney and Grant crawled back into their own bed, shaking their heads in disbelief. Could this get any nuttier? Was Ryan going to end up wrapped around a telephone pole or endangering another driver? They had already walked such a long road with him—watching him flunk out of college, get a DUI and experience all its legal and financial consequences—they could hardly believe it could get any worse. Six years of accumulated stress, seeing their good-natured, gifted son throw everything away, was wearing them down. *How did we get to this point?* Courtney and Grant would often ask themselves. *What did we do wrong? How did he end up like this?* There were no answers, only torment, self-incrimination and a growing sense of hopelessness.

Everybody who knew the family was equally baffled. Couples in their small group at church—people who had seen them respond to all the normal bumps and bruises of raising kids—described their family as loving, stable and strong. Grant's job, the superintendent of a suburban school district, required boat-loads of patience, wisdom and compassion. The same goes for Courtney, a tender-hearted speech therapist.

The nightmare with Ryan started the day they received a call out of the blue from an older woman they knew from town. The news couldn't have been more shocking: this woman's granddaughter had paid a surprise visit to Ryan at school, only to find him passed out drunk in his dorm, with his head by the toilet.

"We were just devastated," Courtney recalls. "We've never had a drop of alcohol in our home. But we found out it's all over the place on campus. Grant called him. Ryan was still in bed. Grant said, 'I'm coming over. Be ready when I get there.'"

That weekend the three of them talked for hours, and before bringing him back to campus, impressed upon him this firm message: "We are not paying for you to go over there and party."

But by the end of the fall semester, it was clear that their warnings had fallen on deaf ears. Ryan wouldn't be returning for the spring term. Instead, he'd be home, working two jobs, trying to earn enough to pay back his parents for the wasted tuition. Working long hours, though, helped Ryan stay sober, and the following fall, with hearts full of hope, and a letter of probationary acceptance, Ryan returned to school. "He was excited about the chance to go back," Courtney said. "So we thought—okay—let's go for it."

The problem was, they learned later, Ryan had come to believe that he *needed* alcohol to come across as fun, talkative and socially comfortable at parties. Hanging out with his old drinking buddies did nothing to dispel that notion and Ryan quickly fell back into his old patterns. At the end of the semester Ryan called saying he had bombed his courses. "He was tearful," Courtney recalls, "He knew he had blown his probation. But he insisted he wasn't drinking, and we chose to believe him."

It was a lie, of course, but Ryan had become quite skillful at that, and for the next few years, managed to hide his drinking from the family, even his brother, with whom he shared an apartment not far from their parents' home. But when Ryan was arrested for DUI, he knew the jig was up—his parents would soon learn of it—because the jailer on duty that night *just so happened* to be a family friend and a member of their church. The second he laid eyes on Ryan, he grabbed him by the arm and jolted him out of his stupor. "What the hell are you doing here?" he demanded. "Do you know what this is doing to your parents?!"

It scared the bejeebers out of Ryan, his parents would later learn, maybe more than the DUI itself. Besides the intimidation, the family connection meant he had to fess up—which he chose to do a few nights later, by calling home in the wee hours, drunk.

"We were stunned and crushed," Courtney said. "Not that we were experts at discerning these things, but we saw no outward signs that he was still drinking. It hit us in the pit of our stomachs— that feeling that our world's just been turned upside down."

Agonizing as that night was, however, Courtney and Grant saw some good in it—God had arranged for Ryan to get caught, to get caught just inside the county with stricter DUI laws *and* to get caught on a night when their friend the jailer was on duty. "I still thank Chris to this day, for giving my son that kick in the back side," Grant said. "I didn't know anything about what Ryan was doing that night, but Chris was there and he did something about it."

"God mercifully caught him," Courtney added. "If he'd never been caught, he could have killed himself or someone else. I know he wouldn't have stopped. We've always been thankful for that."

But for Courtney and Grant, the darkest days were still ahead. Much to their consternation, Ryan didn't seem shaken by the alarming consequences he was facing—even though he had lost his driver's license, was required to attend AA meetings and to submit to periodic drug testing. Plus, he had a mountain of debt from drinking, only made worse by legal expenses.

"It was never as negative to him as it was to us," Grant said. "When I drove him to his court appointments and AA meetings, we'd talk about the seriousness of what was going on. 'This is a mess,' I'd say. 'How are you going to make this right?' He always had a plan. He thought he could work his way out of it on his own."

*If only,* they thought, *Ryan would stop being so darned confident in his own abilities. If only he would start asking the Lord for help.* But whenever they encouraged him this way, Ryan would point back to his own solutions.

"We urged him to see if they had room for him at Twelve Stones,"[2] Courtney said. "It seemed so obvious to us that he needed something residential. He was getting good gospel-centered counseling at church, but once a week wasn't enough. Plus, he was just going through the motions."

Somehow, Ryan managed to pass his periodic drug tests, even though he was still drinking. "We knew because he'd call us in the middle of the night whenever he was drunk," Courtney said.

By that point Grant would pick up the phone saying, "You have five minutes. Say all you've got to say and I'll call you back in the morning when *you* are sleeping." It was just what they needed to curb the late-night drama.

---

2. Twelve Stones Ministries: http://twelvestones.org/

"We laid it out plainly for him," Courtney said. "We'd say, 'Ryan, there is no fruit in your life to lead us to believe that you are saved. None at all. You need to seriously consider whether you are a true believer.'"

Ryan's biggest concern, though, wasn't spiritual, it was financial—and the greater his debt grew, the more hopeless he became. At one point Ryan said to Grant, "Dad, my dream would be that I'd be in a box, living downtown with zero responsibilities."

Hearing these things filled Courtney and Grant with an abiding, penetrating sense of heartache and loss. "We thought Ryan was going to be an engineer," Grant said, "but that dream was lost. And now I didn't know if he would even grow up and be a productive member of society."

Worse than that was the fear that Ryan would never turn back to the Lord. It was one of those dreadful things they had seen happen in other families, despite the parents' persistent prayers. In their exhaustion, the incessant, gravitational pull— the temptation to give in to fear and despair—felt like a magnetic power, incessantly dragging them ever-downward.

One night it all became too much and Courtney woke up with a sense of terror and oppressive anxiety. Waking Grant, she cried, "Would you pray for me? Out loud? Right now?" Of course he did and immediately, Courtney said, "I had the most amazing sense of peace. I was able to lie down and go back to sleep."

Prayer, though it had always been important, had now become central. They pleaded with others for their prayers. They met with other desperate parents twice a month in two separate prayer groups. One day they met with Ryan's counselor. His challenge: Are you willing to pray that God would do whatever it takes to turn Ryan's heart toward himself? *Whatever it takes?* They imagined the disastrous possibilities, but reasoned—nothing is more disastrous than living a life independent of God. *Nothing.*

But they didn't just speak to God; they spoke to *themselves*, reminding themselves over and over what they really believed—that God is sovereign and that He is completely trustworthy. "We knew," Courtney said, "that He might not answer our prayers the way we wanted, but even if that were the case, He would carry us through."

Every day they had to be firm, reminding themselves that, just like Ryan, they had choices to make. What would it be—fear or courage? Resentment or trust? Our desires or His plan? "This was the beginning of my journey," Courtney said, "of *choosing* to trust Him, our sovereign God, even when I didn't feel like it. When I woke up in the morning, I would pray, "God, with your help, I will not let Satan have his way here and steal my joy."

After speaking with Ryan's counselor, they realized they had another hard choice to make—to take to heart this nugget of wisdom: It all boiled down to Ryan's choices. He had made some poor decisions. As to their parenting, the counselor couldn't point to anything big or glaring or stupid. Plus—and this was important—in the Garden of Eden, God was the perfect, loving parent to Adam and Eve, providing everything they needed. Even in this perfect environment, they chose to rebel. They *alone* were responsible.

It was such a mighty effort to weave these truths into their thoughts and speech. But the need, the *dire* need, to partner with each other in the effort drew Courtney and Grant into an ever-increasing intimacy. "When one of us was down," Grant said, "the other would say, 'God is trustworthy. He is sovereign. He is good.' It was a time of deep, deep dependence on God."

While praying for Ryan to change, they also searched their own souls. Grant said, "We really tried to say, 'What do we need to learn from this?'"

"I really believe," Courtney said, "that God worked to make us more gracious and humble with others going through similar things. If we had three kids that had turned out just wonderful, I would have been very prideful. I would have said, 'All you have to do is this, this and this and you won't be having those problems'. I have none of that now. It's all God's grace. It's nothing I did."

For Courtney, growing in humility allowed her to cast off old hesitations about asking for help. One day she dared to make this unwelcome suggestion: "Let's go to the other elders and ask them to lay hands on us and pray—that God would help us persevere and that He would work in Ryan's heart." Over the years, Grant had laid hands and prayed for others hundreds of times before—but never did he consider that he would be the *recipient* of this ministry. "He was not on board with that," Courtney said, smiling.

"It was pride," Grant admitted. "I thought, 'I should know how to handle problems. Here I am, an elder.' I was so reluctant to say, '*I* need to be ministered to and *I* need compassion.' I am much more comfortable *giving* that than getting that. But we surrendered the idea that we had to have the perfect family."

As difficult and humbling as that decision was, Courtney and Grant's time with the elders proved to be the turning point—for within thirty-six hours they saw a change in Ryan that gave them great hope. Once again, the drama unfolded in the middle of the night, but this time Ryan was calling from outside their garage, wanting to come in, but he couldn't remember the security code.

"He had walked from the bar in a snowstorm," Courtney explained, "along this busy road with no sidewalks in the middle of the night. We went running out there. Of course he's freezing cold, wet and drunk. We got blankets and we sat beside him on the couch and talked and prayed. And for the first time ever he said, 'I can't do this anymore. I need help. I want to go to Twelve Stones. I'm ready to go to Twelve Stones.'"

And with those beautiful, simple words, Courtney and Grant knew the Lord had set Ryan's feet on the road to recovery. Together they wept.

Four years later, the photos on Grant's desk tell the rest of the story: one is of an attractive young man and his beaming bride, another of a beautiful grandchild. Ryan, who once idealized a life of zero responsibility, is a fine, upstanding family man, paying the bills and meeting up with his parents at church. The one-time college partier who once equated sober with somber is constantly amazed to hear second-hand that people appreciate his easy laughter, his natural warmth and engaging personality. All this apart from anything found inside a bottle. The thing his parents knew all along, Ryan has discovered for himself.

When Grant looks at those pictures, he remembers the Scripture that encouraged his heart all those years:

> I believe that I shall look upon the goodness of the Lord in the land of the living! Wait for the Lord; be strong and let your heart take courage; wait for the Lord.[3]

---

3. Psalm 27:13-14

"Ryan's recovery didn't happen on our timetable," he said. "But God gave us grace to endure, to be courageous and to wait. And now our lives— they are a picture of redemption. We are different people as a result of this experience. We've changed; Ryan has changed. And we all see God's hand and blessings in everything that happened."

# 7.

# I AM Sufficient

Elliot wasn't sure whether to smile or groan at the photo in his hands—a faded 8 x 10 portrait of his parents on their wedding day, their mocha-brown faces radiant with the joy of being in love. "Mom and Micah were happy once," he said. "It's good to see that."

"But you were too young to remember it," his wife Kim said, seeing his far-off look. "Sifting through all these pictures must be hard for you," she said from her spot across the kitchen table. "It's remarkable your grandpa didn't ditch them after the divorce."

Elliot picked up another photo, this one taken on their honeymoon. "Do you realize it's been twenty-three years since I've seen my biological dad—or even a picture of him?"

"That's crazy," Kim[1] said. She moved to the empty chair next to him and tilted her head against

---

1. Names and identifying details have been changed.

his shoulder. "From what you say, Micah was a good man who got snared by temptation. And as awful as adultery is," she continued, "to sever all paternal contact—what were they thinking?"

Elliot took hold of a lock of her long, silky black hair, an emblem of her Native American heritage, and pulled it through his fingers. "I've been trying to figure that out my whole life. I remember feeling confused—and suspicious. Kids know when adults aren't telling them everything. Why was it that after spending every Sunday afternoon with our biological dad, did we suddenly stop? They said he gave up custody, but why would he? Even then I knew that's not what he wanted. And why, after that, did we never see or hear from him again?"

Elliot flipped through a stack of photos, pulling out the ones with his biological father. *What am I looking for?* he asked himself. *Clues?* Kim once suggested he became a police detective who thrives on solving crime in response to the unresolved mysteries in his past. *Maybe she was right, but what was he supposed to do when the past wouldn't stay in the past?*

"It's hard to describe my family to outsiders," he said. "Mom was very loving, yet bitter beyond belief toward Micah. When she got remarried, it was hard getting used to Warren—he was so authoritarian and controlling. *But* he was willing to adopt Shonda and me, and he did treat us as his kids. So even though my childhood was bizarre, I do love my parents."

"I know you do. But I can also see this has been emotionally draining, pulling together these slides for your grandpa."

"That," Elliot said, pausing as he considered his emotions, "is an understatement. But what could I do? I love him too and all he wants is 'a simple slide show for a simple funeral.'"

"But he gave you too many. We can't sort through them all at once. Remember, he said, 'No rush; I'm not dying tomorrow.' Though with his kind of lymphoma, that could be denial."

"I wish *I* could be in denial. I can barely stand that he's so sick. He and my grandma were a strong, stabilizing influence when Micah vanished from our lives."

"I wish I knew how that happened," Kim said.

*Me too*, Elliot thought. Against his better instincts, he let his mind drift to the past, to memories of hard moments with his mom and Warren: The time his biological dad gave him a set of personalized pencils—a prized possession—and Warren snatched the box and threw it into the fire; the time he brought home a doctor's kit from a Sunday afternoon with Micah, and it too disappeared; the way his mom taught him and Shonda to call their dad "What's-his-name" and forbade them to speak of him; the way Warren exploded in anger when Micah called in the middle of the week; the way the kids at school snickered when his mom and Warren changed his name from Micah to Elliot—since he had been named after his father and they couldn't stand being constantly reminded of the man. Most of all, the way they impressed upon him the sure-fire way he could please them was to treat Micah with scorn and contempt. And the way he did.

"Sometimes," Elliot said, "I wonder—would my dad have ever looked twice at his secretary if he knew infidelity would mean losing his kids?"

"Temptations bury the fine print," Kim said. "Who would want their children raised by another man? Who would choose to not know his grandchildren?"

Suddenly Elliot was struck by a sense of lost time, lost memories, and lost relationships. *These are things nobody can bring back,* Elliot thought. *None of these relationships can be made completely right again. That ship has sailed. The only thing I can do is look forward—to do everything I can to protect my kids from broken relationships, to teach them to live in the light, a life of integrity—no secrets, no lies. And when we fail—grace and forgiveness and restoration.*

Elliot knew that sounded impossible, but he also knew he'd do anything to protect his children from the kind of pain he knew.

Elliot hugged the two pictures to his chest. "Don't let my mother see these—or *any* taken before the divorce. If she knew her parents kept these she'd whip out her scissors and cut my dad out. *And* she'd be hysterical if our kids ever saw them. She always insisted the divorce be a deep, dark secret."

"I was worried about that too," Kim said. "I can just hear the triplets asking, *"Who's that man with Grandma? Where's Grandpa Warren?"*

Kim looked at the clock and quickly began stowing the photos in labeled boxes. "I need to pick up the kids from dance," she said, sliding the boxes toward him. "And then off to the mall for new kid shoes. That'll give you a chunk of time with Antonio."

Elliot felt a little buoyed by the reminder that Antonio, his long-time mentor on the police force, would be arriving soon. When they met last week for breakfast, Elliot shared his grief about his grandfather's diagnosis and the ups and downs of being immersed in his photos and videos.

"Grandpa Kenneth and Grandma Alvera kept a couple of American Quarter Horses on their farm just five miles from our house," Elliot said. "Every chance we got we were over there, riding Chalfant and Chew Magna. Grandpa was a photographer, so he had a lot of pictures and family video from when we were young. He must have kept them out of my mom's sight, because they're all intact—perhaps the only ones in existence of us with our dad.

"But down the road, at *our* house, the whole family worked at erasing this past as if it didn't exist — like we were in a witness relocation program. With scissors, we cut my biological dad out of every photo."

Antonio listened, shaking his head in sadness and disbelief.

"Mom doesn't know this, but Kenneth gave me two shoe boxes filled with thousands of negatives and footage he had shot of Shonda and me when we were young, brushing the horses and playing on the farm. Micah is in there too, holding the reins and teaching us to ride. If I can, I hope to convert a lot over to a DVD for my sister, as a surprise."

"I've heard about your biological father for years," Antonio said. "Now that you have pictures of him, you've got to show me one."

The two men agreed their next meeting would be at Elliot's house.

Elliot set his parents' wedding portrait on the table and carried the boxes into the pantry, sliding them into a dark corner behind the stool. He slid the stool back into the corner and decided on impulse to sit down, thankful for how Kim had turned this space into a little gallery for travel postcards and their kindergarteners' artwork. Alongside the postcards from Ischia—Antonio's favorite Italian island—were purple, green and black crayoned family portraits. Elliot was amused to see their son Richard had drawn him in almost giant-like proportions, his hair black curlicues poking out at odd angles. *Does he think I need a haircut?*

On the shelf to the left, Elliot noticed, was a box of peanut brittle left over from last summer's Cheyenne Frontier Days. *Dad used to bring us there,*

Elliot thought. *Such incredible memories. And yet we were so mean to him, for no reason—no legitimate reason.*

In his mind, he could hear his sister Shonda: "*You* have no reason to feel guilty. Mom and Warren were the ones whose mission in life was to punish Micah. They made us believe he was evil incarnate. They *used* us to make him miserable—so he'd give up custody. We were kids. We did what we were told."

*All of that is true,* Elliot thought, *except for the part about not being culpable. I knew it was wrong.*

Shonda also had an explanation for why their biological dad had *in a dramatic reversal* suddenly given up custody. "He probably got tired of paying child support for the measly amount of time the courts gave him with us."

Elliot weighed that as a possibility, but it seemed out of character. *Dad was generous,* Elliot thought. *He took us to fun restaurants, gave us carefully chosen toys and brought us on vacations and to Cheyenne Frontier Days. It just didn't make sense. And for him to never call or send a card after losing custody—that was out of character too. It was a tangled, messy loose end.*

He noticed he had started clunking his boots together. In his mind, he heard Antonio saying, "*It's not like a father is an inter-changeable part, you know. You can't say, 'No problem: We'll just take Micah out, put Warren in, and let that be the end of it.'*"

Elliot could always count on Antonio for some straight talk. The man had served two tours in

Vietnam. Everyone knew him to be a strong leader and a battle-tested warrior. He was not afraid to speak the truth or fight for justice. More than anything, Elliot appreciated Antonio's way of bringing biblical truth into day-to-day life.

"You take after your dad," Antonio said when he saw the picture. "Long and lean. Thick hair. Possibly a thick head," he said, grinning.

"My head is pretty dense," Elliot said. "This family stuff—the grief and the brokenness and the loose ends—it's too much."

Antonio pulled out a chair, sat down and opened his Bible. "Can I ask you a hard question?" Seeing Elliot nod, he continued. "I know you were under enormous pressure as a child to think and act a certain way. But now that you're an adult, help me understand how you reconcile your faith in Jesus Christ and His redemptive work on the cross with this unreconciled relationship in your life."

Elliot was not surprised to hear Antonio issue such a blunt challenge. It seemed he'd been working up to it for years. The man deserved a straight answer.

"There *is* no way to reconcile it. I just know if I were to reach out to Micah, I don't think I'd survive the fallout."

"Such as…?"

"Ruined relationships," Elliot said, making a stabbing motion toward his chest. "A rerun of all the pain and alienation I grew up with. And here's the worst—if I were to bring all that on my kids. People die from grief, you know."

Antonio swirled the ice around in his water, waiting.

"If I try to reconcile with Micah," Elliot said, "I'm certain Mom and Warren will feel betrayed. It would crush me to hurt them. Warren, in particular, will feel deeply offended, possibly beyond repair."

"It's like a seventh-grade drama," Antonio said.

"I'm used to it. But you can see how they might want to punish me. One scenario: They could take it out on my kids. One day, the kids might get fed up with that and decide that *I'm* to blame for the rift. *Or,* my parents may actively try to turn them against me, like they did with Shonda and me against Micah."

"That's a truckload of pain, I'll grant you that," Antonio said. "Can you see what all of those things have in common?"

"That they'd give me a stroke?" Elliot said.

"They are all choices *someone else* may make in a conflict."

"Choices that affect *me*," Elliot said. "Don't forget that part."

Antonio turned to a bookmarked page. "I think Romans 12:18 speaks to this."

Elliot turned there and read it aloud:

> If possible, so far as it depends on you, live peaceably with all.

"You see that middle part—so far as it depends on you? What if *that* were to become your focus?

Elliot tilted his head and frowned.

"What if, instead of focusing on the fallout—the things *others* may do in a conflict—you were to simply say, 'I am responsible for my own actions, not theirs.'?"

Elliot sighed. "Okay, I get it," he said, sounding defeated, "but like I said—me doing the right thing doesn't mean there won't be fallout."

"True. And then what? That's where faith comes in—to trust Him, to know there are blessings in obedience, even when it costs us."

"At this point," Elliot said, his voice rising, "I wonder if I have any faith at all. I have lived most of my life separated from my biological dad. This feels crazy, almost self-destructive, to now risk losing my mom and step-dad—and down the road possibly losing the loving relationship I have with our kids. And don't forget. I won't have my grandfather for long."

"I know. I'm very sorry," Antonio said. "You are facing a hard choice. Perhaps a test."

Elliot nodded and re-read the verse, trying to figure the odds of this turning out well. He watched Antonio examine again his parents' wedding portrait, then fiddle absent-mindedly with the elastic band on his journal. Even now the shrapnel scars on Antonio's hands and neck were noticeable. They reminded him of the stories—graphic stories—Antonio would occasionally tell about Vietnam:

about fallen comrades on the battle field, about carrying them in his arms, and about taking their dog tags and contacting their wives. Elliot always came away from those conversations with a better understanding of what it means to do hard things in life, to accept there are many things we can't control and won't understand, that there's always a sting and we always grieve, but there is One—Jesus—who will ultimately take the sting away.

"Antonio," he said, "I'm dying here. I love my parents and my children. And I know God wants me to reconcile with Micah. I need to wrestle this out. You'd better be praying for me."

Elliot wiped the condensation from the study window and watched his old friend tread carefully over the dusting of snow to his car. *Had Antonio developed a limp?* The man had a will of iron. It reminded Elliot of the times Antonio described his struggles to surrender his will and agenda to the Lord. *That's what I want to do, Lord,* Elliot prayed, *You know what I am going through right now. You wrestled—in agony. And yet, ultimately, You surrendered Your will.*[2]

Elliot was absorbed at his desk when his daughter Annie appeared in the doorway, cowgirl hat in hand. As soon as she caught his eye, she donned her hat and danced across the room in the country style she'd learned in class. Elliot applauded, and in a matter of seconds, she was in his lap. "Well, look

---

2. In the Garden of Gethsemane, Jesus prayed, "Not as I will, but as you will." Matthew 26:39

who it is: Annie Oakley in a new pair of cowgirl boots. *Red* this time!"

"That's not my name, Daddy," she said, grinning.

"Are you sure?" he said, tapping her boots together.

"Tell me," he said, handing her a small stack of index cards from the desk, "can you find the word *love* in this first Bible verse?"

While Annie traced her fingers across the words, Elliot sent Kim a quick text: *Forgot photo on table.* She replied: *Stashed it in the kitchen desk.*

*Lord,* he prayed, *how do we not perpetuate a culture of secrecy here?*

"Can I read to you Annie? Can you listen very quietly?"

Annie put her hat on the desk, pressed her lips together and set her gaze on the cards. Kim had come in and leaned against the doorframe, listening.

"I just want to share with you the first three of these Bible verses here."

> He has told you, O man, what is good; and what does the LORD require of you but to do justice and to love kindness, and to walk humbly with your God?[3]

> So if you are offering your gift at the altar and there remember that your brother has something against you, leave your gift there before the altar and go. First be reconciled to your brother, and then come and offer

---

3. Micah 6:8

your gift.[4]

Whoever loves father or mother more than me is not worthy of me, and whoever loves son or daughter more than me is not worthy of me.[5]

Elliot rested his chin on the top of Annie's head and wrapped his arms around her tiny five-year-old frame. She started to sing, under her breath, a tune from her class. Her little red boots tilted this way and that till finally she wriggled her way off his lap, trilled a goodbye and flitted out of the room, taking her daddy's heart with her.

"Seriously scared that I'm not worthy," he said, pulling Annie's hat atop one knee.

After supervising the kids' baths and story time, Elliot headed directly to the master bedroom, eager to meditate on the verses he had written out.

"Do you remember that sermon last fall about reconciling?" he said when Kim came to bed.

Kim chuckled. "Who could forget it? I know it made some people mad."

Their pastor, nearing the end of a sermon on Matthew 5:23-24, exhorted the congregation to take the verse literally, in that very moment. "Beloved, can we see the priority Jesus gives to reconciling? It comes *before* worship. Why not do what He says right now? I invite you to stand up, walk out, and make that call, or simply walk across the aisle, or

---

4. Matthew 5:23-24
5. Mathew 10:37

turn to the person sitting next to you. Go ahead. The praise band will play while you take Jesus at His word."

"I should've gotten up that day," he said, tapping the cards on his thigh. "Plain and simple, I didn't trust God enough to risk upsetting my parents—as if pleasing them is everything."

He reached out, took hold of her hand, brought it to his lips and kissed it. "And the kids too," he said softly. "They are so precious, if my actions brought pain into their lives—how could I live with that? How does a protective dad trust God with his kids?"

Kim sat up straight and poked Elliot's shoulder. "I remember once you told me that you wouldn't trade your childhood because, as painful as it was, God used it to *forge* you into a stronger person, like a tool He can use for the kingdom. Remember how you said that was the meaning of *'Count it all joy'*?"[6]

"I said that?" Elliot said, smiling.

"Won't God do the same with our kids? Don't they *need* to have trials and to suffer—for the same reasons you did?"

"My wise and wonderful wife! If I ever have a nightmare about red cowgirl boots being thrown into the fire, or if anything like that happens in real life, please remind me of that. Seriously."

---

6. "Count it all joy, my brothers and sisters, when you meet trials of various kinds, for you know that the testing of your faith produces steadfastness. And let steadfastness have its full effect, that you may be perfect and complete, lacking in nothing" (James 1:2-4).

"If they decide to go that route," she said, "we'll still be better off than disobeying."

"Listen," he said, standing up and setting the stack of cards beside her. "I'm headed to the kitchen for a minute. Could you read the rest of these verses? I'm praying, 'Help my unbelief.'"[7]

> But he said to me, "My grace is sufficient for you, for my power is made perfect in weakness." Therefore I will boast all the more gladly of my weaknesses, so that the power of Christ may rest upon me. For the sake of Christ, then, I am content with weaknesses, insults, hardships, persecutions, and calamities. For when I am weak, then I am strong.[8]

> For am I now seeking the approval of man, or of God? Or am I trying to please man? If I were still trying to please man, I would not be a servant of Christ.[9]

> For my father and my mother have forsaken me, but the LORD will take me in.[10]

> "Why do you call me 'Lord, Lord', and not do what I tell you?"[11]

> Trust in the LORD with all of your heart and do not lean on your own understanding. In all of your ways,

---

7. Mark 9:24
8. 2 Corinthians 12:9-10
9. Galatians 1:10
10. Psalm 27:10
11. Luke 6:46

acknowledge him, and he will make straight your paths.[12]

'These are great verses,' Kim said when he returned, this first one especially."

Their prayers that night, and for the next four weeks, were full of petitions for grace to believe, trust, and obey.

When Elliot found himself awake in the middle of the night, he would often imagine how he wanted to put together his Grandpa Kenneth's slides. One Saturday he decided to tackle it, and was surprised to see that he felt a measure of peace. *That is God's grace, and nothing else,* he thought. *Thank you, Lord.*

When he was finished, he made the DVD he had planned for Shonda, ninety minutes of long-forgotten images of their time on the farm and with Micah. *Despite a lot of hard circumstances, God blessed us with a lot of good memories.* He put the DVD on the bench by the back door, hoping he could bring it over the following week.

One night, Elliot slept through his daughter Theresa's nightmare and the rumble and scraping of an early morning snowplow.

"You've turned a corner, haven't you?" Kim said one morning when he came down the stairs and two-stepped over to the kitchen desk, index cards in hand. "What's happened?"

"Come over to here, my darlin'," he said, affecting a cowboy's twang, "and I'll tell you. I believe this

---

12. Proverbs 3:5-6

drawer even contains a visual aid." He pulled his parents' wedding portrait out and set in on top of the desk. "*This,*" he said tapping the picture with a hint of pique, "represents all my anxiety and fear, all my lack of faith. And *these,*" he said, covering the photo with his Bible verses, "represent me deciding to believe God. It gives me great joy to report: *Faith* is what's happened. Faith *prevails over* the circumstances. No matter what happens, His grace is sufficient. In insults or persecution, or calamities, He'll sustain us, just like He says."

Kim touched the cards, noticing they were two layers deep covering the photo. "That's a lot of faith you've got right there. Thank you, Lord!" She opened her arms wide. "Let me hug you, mighty warrior. What's your plan?"

"To get this behind me as soon as possible. I found Micah's email online and shot him a note just now. As soon as he responds—*if* he responds— I'll go tell my parents."

"Are you ready for that?" Kim asked.

"I've outlined some points in my journal, but no matter how I word it, this is going to be painful for them. They won't understand my desire to follow the Scriptures. But I hope they'll sense I'm coming with the right heart and a desire to honor them by being honest and transparent. I'll have to count on God to fill in the pieces with Warren because this needs to be done. I can't live a life of authenticity without reaching out to Micah and trying to reconcile the parts I might reconcile."

Later that week, Elliot left his parents' house with a heavy heart. "They were distraught," he told Kim when he got home. "They kept saying they didn't understand, and it wasn't necessary, and why would I think I needed to seek Micah's forgiveness? I hugged them and was tearful and told them, Warren especially, 'It doesn't mean I don't love you or appreciate what you've done by taking me in and raising me as yours. I'll always consider you my dad. But this is something, in the name of Jesus, I need to do. I had a responsibility in this and I don't want to leave any stone unturned.' They both looked at me blankly, as if I were speaking a foreign language."

Together, Elliot and Kim grieved the reality, sitting quietly in front of the fire, occasionally passing each other a Bible verse, and offering up silent prayers for everyone involved. *I sure hope my luncheon date with Micah is worth all this heartache,* Elliot thought.

Three days later, Elliot left his time with his biological father in a sensory overload, not sure if he could *or wanted* to believe the things he heard.

"Prepare yourselves for a shock, ladies," Elliot said as he entered the kitchen, knowing Kim and Shonda would be waiting for a full report.

"That sounds ominous," Kim said. "What happened?"

Elliot shed his coat and headed for the coffee pot. "Micah said that when Shonda and I were younger, some men muscled their way into his house, beat him with baseball bats and threw him down the basement stairs."

"Are you serious?" Kim said. "Who would want to hurt Micah?"

"He told me these men threatened his family and beat him unconscious," Elliot said.

"Tell me you're making this up," Shonda said from her bar stool. "You're saying *our mild-mannered, accountant father* was attacked by a bunch of thugs?"

"That's what he told me," Elliot said.

Kim motioned everyone to the family room and curled up in her recliner. Shonda headed to the fireplace and took hold of the poker.

"I want to hear everything," Kim said. "Please start from the beginning."

"You know my goal was to apologize," Elliot said, sinking with a sigh into his recliner. "I told him I realized I had treated him unfairly when I was young—that I'd taken Mom's side in the custody battle. And that he had been a good dad to us, and that I regretted the pain I had caused him."

"Whew," Kim said, exhaling deeply. "Was that hard?"

"Actually, it felt really good. He was gracious and said that he was fine and could see that I was being manipulated—that we both were being manipulated," he said, looking over at Shonda.

Shonda poked a new log so hard it tumbled to the back, out of reach of the flames.

"It must have shocked him to hear from you," Kim said.

"He did ask what brought this about. I said, 'Dad, in the Old Testament, there's a verse that tells us to do justice, love kindness, and walk humbly with God—all things I failed to do as a twelve-year-old.'

'Oh, Micah 6:8,' he said.

'You know it?' I said, surprised. I felt bad—in his eyes I could see we were thinking the same thing: *So many years have passed without any contact. And now here we are, a father and son who do not know each other.*

"Almost in a whisper he said, 'Did you say there were *two* verses?'

"I was astounded the way this conversation was going, but I pressed on. 'It's from the book of Romans.'

If possible, so far as it depends on you, live peaceably with all.[13]

"He nodded, seeming like he knew that one too. I told him a friend of mine pointed out that my faith in Christ compelled me to reach out to him."

"How did he take all that?" Kim said. "If I were him, I think I would have cried."

"He did, but not that second. A minute later I showed him some pictures of the triplets. 'Oh, son,' he said, 'They are beautiful! I had no idea I had

---

13.Romans 12:18

grandkids out there. And my goodness—triplets!' he said, with big tears rolling down his cheeks."

"Poor Dad," Shonda said. "He lost out on so much."

"I know. But it was as if seeing the photos set off a trigger, because then he started telling me about the assault. He rolled up his sleeves and his pants legs and showed me foot-long scars, surgical scars where he needed plates and screws.

"He said it happened when I was twelve, when Mom and Warren were in the thick of the custody battle, and things were so hostile. He said these men beat him within an inch of his life.

"And before he blacked out they got in his face and through gritted teeth said, 'Stay away from Elliot and Shonda! If you ever try to contact them again, we'll be back. And you won't live to tell the tale. And then what do you think we'll do to that fine china *wife* of yours—and your little *children*?'"

Shonda and Kim gasped in unison.

"That's horrible!" Shonda said. "Did he report it? No, he wouldn't have. He couldn't have."

"No. He dared not risk his wife or children's lives."

Kim suddenly sat up in her recliner, pushing the foot rest to the floor. "This is astounding. Now the great mystery is solved! If it's true, now you know why he didn't continue to fight for custody—why he disappeared so suddenly from your lives. Doesn't that bring you some comfort? He feared for the lives of his new family!"

"I don't know where I stand on that," Elliot said. "I hardly know him—certainly not well enough to know if he's telling the truth. But if he is—think about what that means—that Warren is capable of that kind of brutality. And possibly that Mom was a part of it. I really don't want to believe that."

"*I* believe it," Shonda said. "Remember when it came out somehow that he and his hoodlum teenage friends killed their neighbors' pets—for fun?"

"He's changed a lot since then," Elliot said. "He has a lot of redeeming qualities."

"As far as I can see," Kim said, "there would be only one reason for Micah to make this up: to play the victim and excuse himself for abandoning you."

"That sounds far-fetched," Shonda said. "He didn't fake the scars. How else could he have sustained those injuries?"

"Who knows?" Elliot said. "But there's one last thing. Before we left the restaurant, Micah told me, when he is gone, all of the details of this are going to come out—that he has a lockbox with some documentation or something and everyone will know the truth."

"A lockbox?" Kim said. "I don't understand. Like with medical records, or what?"

"I don't know. I asked him some questions, but he was evasive. It became clear he didn't want to tell me any more."

"So, we're left now with *what*—more mystery?" Shonda said, her voice pitched. "This makes me want to scream! How can you be so calm?"

"I wasn't expecting anything *from* him," Elliot said. "I just wanted to alleviate the pain I caused, if I could."

"Elliot, I'm sorry," Shonda said. "I don't think I can stay. I feel like I'm going to burst into tears any second."

Elliot and Kim rushed to her side.

"They robbed us," Shonda said, the tears welling up in her eyes and spilling down her cheeks. "They robbed us of a relationship with our father. Nothing can bring back those years. *Nothing.*"

"It is devastating," Elliot said, "to think what might be true. And it's devastating to think how this might lead to more broken relationships."

"*Might?*" Shonda said, twisting away. "Right now, I can't imagine any way we could continue as before. Can *you?*" She returned the poker to its stand and headed toward the back door.

"My mind is too jumbled to say. I need to pray about it." He followed her as she threw on her coat and boots. "Don't leave, Shonda. Let's process this together."

"Maybe later, brother. I love you. I love you both. I just need to be alone, okay?"

The echo of the slammed door hung in the air. A little stunned, Elliot and Kim stood in the back hallway, watching the snow spitting from under

Shonda's wheels. In ten seconds, she was out of sight. Elliot dropped heavily onto the bench. Next to him, the DVD he made for Shonda seemed to mock him and his intentions of sharing happy family memories. "What am I going to do with this now?" Elliot said. "Was it a mistake telling her everything Micah said? Is there any way I could have done this differently?"

"Don't worry," Kim said. "You did right. Remember what you decided to believe: His grace is sufficient for hardships and calamities."

As the weeks passed, the stack of index cards grew. And Elliot, who had always enjoyed reading and writing short stories, decided to write one about this experience. The protagonist realized his "Garden of Gethsemane moment"—surrendering his children to God's care—was a warm-up, God preparing him for greater hardships and calamities to come, as they surely would in this broken world. Writing was therapeutic, and in the back of his mind was Shonda.

More weeks passed and Elliot and Kim discussed how to follow up with Micah, finally deciding to invite him and his wife to come meet the kids. "Listen, Dad," Elliot said on the phone, "at some point, when the kids are older, and can be trusted to *not* say to Warren, 'You're not our *real* grandpa,' Kim and I will explain who you are. For now, we're referring to you as a family friend." Micah said he understood, agreed to sign any cards appropriately, and asked about the kids' interests.

Despite a lot of apprehension, it turned out to be a pleasant afternoon. Micah arrived with the exact-right presents; he read stories, and the kids seemed to enjoy him. Elliot recorded video.

*Is this going to be a regular event?* Elliot asked himself. He wasn't sure. He was glad they all made the effort, but there was something about Micah's demeanor that gave Elliot the sense that he was not inclined to be woven into the fabric of their lives. *You can't put Humpty Dumpty back together again,* Elliot thought, *not this side of heaven.*

Likewise, Elliot's conversations with his mom were strained and awkward. And Warren, though he would deny it, was giving Elliot the cold shoulder. *Either he feels I've been disloyal and ungrateful,* Elliot thought, *or he's afraid he's been exposed.*

"I'm in a lose-lose situation here," Elliot told Antonio one day at breakfast. "I lose my relationship with Warren if I believe he orchestrated that beating, and I lose my relationship with Micah if I believe he is lying."

"That's a hard place," Antonio said. "What now?"

"I keep wondering if there's something I need to do. Do I tell Warren what Micah said? Am I called to exhort him to repent? Do I break off contact if he denies it?"

"This is not your battle," Antonio said. "This is between Micah and Warren. If you sense that Micah is telling the truth and has not forgiven Warren, the most you can do is encourage him to go work it out. The rest is between him and the Lord."

Elliot nodded, closed his eyes and exhaled deeply, tilting his head side to side, releasing the tension in his neck.

Antonio opened his Bible. "Have you read Psalm 46 lately?" he asked.

"It's been a while," Elliot said. He turned there and read it silently. He read it again, focusing on certain verses.

> God is our refuge and strength, a very present help in trouble. Therefore we will not fear though the earth gives way, though the mountains be moved into the heart of the sea,[14]

> The nations rage, the kingdoms totter; he utters his voice, the earth melts. The LORD of hosts is with us; the God of Jacob is our fortress.[15]

> Be still and know that I am God.[16]

When he got to the end, he looked up at Antonio with wide eyes. "*That* is food to my soul. I needed that."

When Elliot got to the station, he pulled into his parking spot and took his journal out of his backpack. "Be still and know I am God," he wrote in letters so large they covered the entire page. On

---

14. Psalm 46:1-2
15. Psalm 46:6-7
16. Psalm 46:10a

the opposite page he wrote, "Lord, I am going to put this situation in your lap. This is not mine to figure out. I may never know what happened back then, but You do, and You are a God of justice. I can just abide and be still."

It was time to get inside but something in his backpack kept him from sliding his journal back in. *Oh, right, Shonda's DVD,* he thought. *I need to see if she's free tonight.*

She was, and she was overjoyed to get the DVD. Together, they watched the home movies, happy to be reminded of positive childhood experiences. *Thank you, Lord,* Elliot found himself thinking as he watched her joyful expression. *Please help Shonda. Please give her the healing and peace that You've given me.*

Later that evening, thinking about what he could incorporate into his short story, he picked up his pen again. "We serve a God who has proven himself faithful and trustworthy. Through the things we fear the most, He is there. He is for us, not against us.[17] Everything is not wrapped up with a bow, but I can trust in the assurance of things hoped for, the conviction of things I can't see.[18] When Christ returns, He will restore and redeem all these broken things.[19] Until then, I am convinced His grace is sufficient.[20] I am at total peace."

---

17.Romans 8:31

18.Hebrews 11:1

19.Revelation 21:5

20.2 Corinthians 12:9

# 8.

# I AM the Suffering Servant

"Pain is such a problem," I said one morning as I came into the kitchen. My husband Tom looked up from his tablet, took in my disheveled appearance and set his spoon back in the bowl.

"Why didn't you call me?" he said, furrowing his thick Italian brows. He stood, tugged my waistband up, and yanked the hem of my shirt down a tad harder than necessary. "I can help you, you know."

"It's humiliating," I said. "I want to pull my pants up myself."

He grunted, took the hairbrush and clip out of my hands, spun me around, and adroitly brushed and clipped my hair in the back. *He's gotten way too good at this,* I thought.

"What time is your physical therapy appointment today?" he said, adjusting the clip.

"I cancelled it." I felt his hands drop onto my shoulders and heard him take in a deep breath.

"Look," he said, turning me to face him. "I *want* you to go. I've got the finances figured out. You need to get better."

"What's the use?" I said. "It's only making me worse."

It was a conversation we had had before, several times, in the months since I was diagnosed with frozen shoulder—a not entirely accurate name, given that my left shoulder felt as if a team of microscopic men stood with blowtorches at the ready, poised to fire up the instant I moved.

"This has gone on long enough," he said. "Why won't you consider surgery?"

"Of course I'm considering it. But I also know we have two tuition bills coming up. And what about your car?"

"My car will be fine. Jerry said it'd last the winter."

"And the tuition?"

"I'm telling you, I've been looking it all over. I'll show you the numbers tonight. We can make it work."

"Does 'making it work' mean seeing you stress over every purchase?" I asked. "That's far worse than me being a one-armed bandit." It was my turn to give a hard look. He lowered his chin, and sighed.

"I'm not going to be stressed," he said. "God's helped me with that."

*I hope that's true*, I thought. *The last thing we need is more stress.* Over the last months, so much scar tissue had formed over the joint that my left arm was essentially pinned to my side. *Be patient with it,* the first two doctors said. *No need to rush to surgery,* they said. *The disease will "run its course": A gradual shrinking in the range of motion; then a long, frozen stage; followed by a slow thawing-out stage. Consistent physical therapy advised.*

The medical journals I sleuthed out confirmed what I was hearing. *And* studies showed surgical patients had the same long-term outcomes as the wait-it-out crowd. At the time, it seemed like a no brainer—wait it out. But for me, and my perpetually frozen, refusing-to-thaw shoulder, it was the wrong choice. After many months of agony, and many dollars spent on ineffective therapy, it became clear surgery was my only option.

Thankfully, Tom was right. Looking at the numbers that night, I agreed; if our trusty mechanic was right, we could go ahead with the surgery. The next day I called the shoulder surgeon's office, beyond eager to get this thing resolved.

"The doctor's next opening is late November," the admin said.

*Three weeks from now,* I thought. "Do you keep a waiting list in case of cancellations?" I asked.

"I could take your name, Mrs. Cappucci, but I should tell you" she said, "people fly in from across the country to see Dr. Agrawal. We don't get many cancellations."

"Okay," I said, "so when could we schedule the surgery?" I heard her clicking her keyboard.

"Late December is his earliest opening," she said. "Sorry, Mrs. Cappucci. In the meantime, we request you complete the medical history forms on our web site. Perhaps your primary care physician can prescribe some pain medication for you?"

I thanked her, ended the call, and fetched the long dowel that I used to do PT exercises. *I think she means "so-called pain medicine"*, I thought. *More like a placebo for all the difference it makes.* Doing my best to raise the dowel, I ruminated: *If only we could have known sooner it would come to this. I could have had the surgery before Tom's car started to fall apart.*

Later that afternoon I started filling out medical history forms. Half-way through, I texted Tom with a question about his company's insurance coverage. His response confused me: "Waiting to hear what Jerry says. Will explain tonight."

I didn't want to speculate what that meant, but was happy to get off the computer. For the past week, I'd been looking for a block of time to bake and deliver lemon squares to the new neighbors down the block. Also, I'd been wanting to get back to my audio book; listening while I baked was a great distraction from whatever mysterious thing Tom couldn't tell me in a text. An hour later, walking home from the neighbor's house, I felt sad about the state of our world—where a new neighbor would act suspicious and reluctant to accept baked goods from a woman *claiming to live down the block.* In my mind, I pictured her trying to confirm my identity online, or simply tossing the lemon squares in the trash. I understood, but it was still sad.

As I pulled a few flyers from the mailbox, I could hear Tom's aged engine coming down the street. *That's the sound of guilt,* I thought. *His car sounds like that because of my shoulder.* But seeing Tom's facial expression through the windshield jolted me out of my defeatist self-talk.

"What's wrong?" I asked as he was getting out of his car.

"Let's go inside."

*Good grief,* I thought. *If this were a scene in a movie, he'd be telling me to knock back a stiff drink while directing me to a chair. Did he get fired?*

"The car sounded worse than usual this morning," he said, "so I left work early and had Jerry check the axel again."

I shuddered, picturing his thirty-minute highway commute downtown and back. "I don't understand why you won't take my car," I said. "I didn't go anywhere today. What if the axel broke on the highway?"

"What if it broke down *on you*?" he said.

I poured two glasses of lemonade. "Knock that back," I said, smiling, and sliding a glass his way. We'd had this conversation before too.

"Anyway," he said, "It'll cost us two thousand to keep it running."

"Yowzers," I said. "Not worth it."

He inhaled, crossed his arms behind his head, and arched his back. "I really didn't want to add a car loan to our tuition bills."

"If that's going to stress you out," I said, "I'll drive you on the days I need the car."

He looked at me with big, uncertain eyes. After a long pause, he exhaled and said, "God will work this out."

We were back to my profound and penetrating insight: *Pain is such a problem.*

As I set out to research cars and car loans, I thought back over months and months of physical, emotional and spiritual angst. *God must have had a good purpose for not directing me to surgery sooner, but what was it? We could have saved so much money, and it would have spared me so much pain if—at any one of my medical appointments—God had whispered in someone's ear: She has a pinched nerve; get her into surgery.* But far beyond the physical pain, and miles beyond the financial pain, was something so intense, I could only hint about it in my conversations with Tom: the pressing sense that God had some grand—but as of yet, undisclosed—purpose in this trial. But what? I was a counselor at church. Back when I was preparing for my certification exams[1], I learned that suffering has many purposes:

- It helps us become more Christ-like in our character.[2]

---

1. The study of God's attributes, including sovereignty, is a part of the curriculum developed by the Association of Certified Biblical Counselors.

2. Romans 8:28-29

- It reorients our priorities, away from the allurements of this world and toward knowing Christ more intimately.[3]
- It creates a desire to further the Kingdom of God, working for the good of others, society, and the spread of the Gospel.[4]
- It can free us from the idea that God exists to be our assistant, someone we allow in our lives so long as He helps bring about our agenda. We come to love Him for Himself, not merely for what He can give us.[5]
- It prepares us to minister to others.[6]
- It helps us identify and turn from idols in our hearts and other ungodly thoughts and deeds.[7]
- It multiplies the glory and joy we will experience in heaven.[8]
- It can make us more resilient, producing endurance, character and hope.[9]

As I thought about this list, knowing it was far from comprehensive, I had to admit, any one of them—or all of them—could be the reason for my suffering. Some of them scared me—especially the possibility this was discipline. *Had I made an idol*

---

3. Philippians 3:7-11

4. *Walking with God through Pain and Suffering*, p. 165-166, Penguin Group, 2013

5. Job 2:9-10; See Elisabeth Elliot's book, *No Graven Image*

6. 2 Corinthians 1:4

7. Psalm 119:75

8. 2 Corinthians 4:17-18

9. Romans 5:3

*out of my desire for a functioning, pain-free shoulder, and the active lifestyle I had?* I remembered a Tim Keller quote I had taped to a shelf in my pantry: "Anything you add to Jesus as a requirement for being happy will strangle you. Until God breaks the strangle, you'll be miserable."[10]

Maybe God's purpose in my pain was to free me from thinking I needed anything in addition to Jesus. *Could I lead a joyful, grateful, fruitful, God-honoring life in my current condition?* Honestly, I couldn't imagine it—and that terrified me. *Was my trust in God that fragile?*

As a reminder of God's goodness and sovereignty, I read and re-read the index cards propped up on the kitchen window:

The LORD is righteous in all his ways and kind in all his works.[11]

Everything is necessary that he sends. Nothing is necessary that he withholds.[12]

God in His love always wills what is best for us. In His wisdom, He always knows what is best, and in His sovereignty, He has the power to bring it about.[13]

10. Timothy Keller, https://twitter.com/DailyKeller, 6/4/15

11. Psalm 145:17

12. John Newton, Letter IV, Dependence on Christ-God's Prescriptions, www.puritansermons.com/newton

13. An unattributed quote from *Trusting God: Even when Life Hurts* by Jerry Bridges (NavPress 1988), p.17

For the LORD God is a sun and shield; the LORD bestows favor and honor. No good thing does he withhold from those who walk uprightly.[14]

I needed these assurances, and would rehearse them often—as when barraged with these disturbing thoughts:

It grieved me to burden Tom, so I tried to hide how much I was struggling.

Guilt-laden accusations harassed me like a swarm of hornets. *How did this happen, Janice? Were you careless at the gym? Have you been eating high-inflammatory foods? Have you been slouching over your keyboard?* I wondered if a frontal lobotomy would muzzle my torturers.

I feared the intense pain would drive me insane or lead me to dependency on narcotics.

More often than was probably healthy, I asked myself if this was a discipline issue. Had I been stubborn about some issue? Did I *require* this severe level of discipline? "Be not like a horse or a mule, without understanding, which must be curbed with bit and bridle..."[15] I wept at the possibility that this warning applied to me.

But maybe this wasn't really about discipline; maybe it was more about *intimacy*. I thought about my favorite verse, the intimacy David described there, and the yearning it produced in me to know the Lord like that.

---

14. Psalm 84:11

15. Psalm 32:9 The verse follows a promise that God will teach and lead us.

You make known to me the path of life;

In your presence there is fullness of joy;

At your right hand are pleasures forevermore.[16]

What if my trial, all this suffering, was *a gift*—a light and momentary affliction designed to clear the way to the path of life, fullness of joy and eternal pleasures at His right hand? It was such a hopeful concept. Instantly, my thoughts jumped to Paul's encouragement to the Corinthians:

> So we do not lose heart. Though our outer self is wasting away, our inner self is being renewed day by day. For this light momentary affliction is preparing for us an eternal weight of glory beyond all comparison, as we look not to the things that are seen but to the things that are unseen. For the things that are seen are transient, but the things that are unseen are eternal.[17]

It was an encouragement *and* a challenge: Where were my eyes focused—on the things I could see, the transient things? Or things unseen and eternal?

I also found myself lingering over the way Jesus questioned Saul on the road to Damascus. Hell-bent on persecuting Christians, Saul was knocked over and stopped dead in his tracks when Jesus asked, "Saul, Saul, why are you persecuting *me*?"[18] If Jesus felt the persecution of Saul's victims, and of the martyrs who would follow, did that really

---

16. Psalm 16:11

17. 2 Corinthians 4:16-18

18. Acts 9:4 (emphasis added)

mean Jesus was in agony along with *me*? The cynic in me judged it as way too sentimental to be true. After all, my suffering could hardly compare with theirs; an inflamed shoulder was a far cry from being stoned to death, fed to the lions or dipped in pitch to light the city.

But I couldn't ignore the other references that pointed to intimacy. Peter told the persecuted Christians to rejoice insofar as they shared in Christ's sufferings,[19] and Paul claimed that he suffered the loss of all things *joyfully* for the sake of greater intimacy with Christ.[20] So, not only does Jesus feel *our* suffering, as He indicated to Saul on the road to Damascus, but when we suffer we are connected to *Christ's* sufferings. What a mystery that was to me! At the time, I was a long way from understanding "the fellowship of sharing in His sufferings"[21] in more than an academic way.

I searched for models of suffering well, people who didn't appear to be like a horse or a mule, people who *yielded* their natural desire for good health to God's sovereign will. One day, I stumbled upon the story of Blaise Pascal, a 17th century theologian and mathematician who contracted a fatal illness *in his 30's*. Hear how he spoke to the Lord about the matter:

> I ask you neither for health nor for sickness, for life nor for death; but that you may dispose of my health and

---

19.1 Peter 4:12-13
20.Philippians 3:8-10
21.Philippians 3:10

my sickness, my life and my death, for your glory... You alone know what is expedient for me; you are the sovereign master, do with me according to your will. Give to me, or take away from me, only conform my will to yours. I know but one thing, Lord, that it is good to follow you, and bad to offend you. Apart from that, I know not what is good or bad in anything. I know not which is most profitable to me, health or sickness, wealth or poverty, nor anything else in the world. That discernment is beyond the power of men or angels, and is hidden among the secrets of your providence, which I adore, but do not seek to fathom.[22]

Pascal's attitude stunned me. Whereas my fingers were clenched tight around the life I wanted—the life I *had*—Pascal's hands, it seemed, were open, wide open to whatever God willed.

Ammunition for the battle arrived in the form of another old saint's[23] exhortations:

The one misery of man is self-will; the one secret of blessedness is the conquest over our own wills. To yield them up to God is rest and peace. What disturbs us in this world is not "trouble" but our opposition to trouble. The true source of all that frets and irritates, and wears away our lives, is not in external things, but in the resistance of our wills to the will of God expressed by external things.

---

22. Blaise Pascal (1623–1662). Minor Works. The Harvard Classics. 1909–14.

23. Alexander MacLaren, 1826-1910

I squirmed and winced at the baldness of his message. The man seemed to know me.

One evening, seeing my weariness as I pulled an ice pack out of the freezer, Tom took me in his arms and said, "I'm praying that God would give that pain to me instead."

"No way!" I cried. "That's insane! I wouldn't wish this on my worst enemy!"

"But I hate to see you in such agony," he said, kissing my temples. "I would take that pain for you."

I knew he would—and it made me weep. I was aghast at the thought of this dear man suffering for the sake of my relief, even hypothetically. *What was he thinking?*

As I pondered these things—not just Tom's prayer, but the whole frozen shoulder saga—I started to remember, bit by bit, a prayer of my own. A few weeks ago, I asked God to help me comprehend the breadth and length and height and depth of Christ's love for me.[24] I had almost forgotten about it, but apparently God had not. Like a florescent light flickering to brightness, my dim memory was now flashing neon, as if God had taken my head in His hands, knocked the glasses off my face with a single, massive swipe, clearing the way for me to see the purpose for my pain. This was all His doing—all *orchestrated* to give me a clearer picture of His love for

---

24. Paul prayed this for his friends in Ephesus, knowing that, without it, they would be utterly ill-equipped to live the Christian life. (See Ephesians 3:18)

me. There was something about imagining myself moving freely while Tom clutched his shoulder in pain, or in contortions trying to take off his coat, that intensified—exponentially—the horror that I felt when I now envisioned Jesus on His way to the Cross. There was nothing hypothetical about *His* scourging, *His* thorns or *His* nails. *They were real.*

To think of the price He paid: The absolute degradation! The shame! The scandalous injustice! The physical torture! And worst of all, the emotional agony of suffering the Father's wrath! None of which He deserved. But he took all of it, to spare me! *Why had this never struck me so viscerally before?* Familiarity, to be sure, but there was more; my life before frozen shoulder had been too cushy for me to really "get" His suffering. But now—*now*—my relatively pint-sized pain was ushering me into this unimaginable intimacy of understanding *His* pain, *His* sacrifice, and most importantly, *His* deep, deep love for me. *This* is what Paul was talking about; *this* is what made all the worldly treasures he left behind pale in comparison; *this* was the fellowship of sharing in Christ's suffering.

All that intensity gushed to the surface, unbidden, one day in a neighborhood Bible study when our discussion reminded me of the passage in Isaiah about the Suffering Servant. We all turned to the 53rd chapter and as I spoke the words that prophesized about Jesus and His crucifixion, my mind's eye was seeing, with fresh vision, that hill far away.

> He was despised and rejected by men,
> a man of sorrows and acquainted with grief;
> and as one from whom men hide their faces
> he was despised, and we esteemed him not.
> Surely he has borne our griefs
> and carried our sorrows;
> yet we esteemed him stricken,
> smitten by God, and afflicted.
> But he was pierced for our transgressions;
> he was crushed for our iniquities;
> upon him was the chastisement that brought us peace,
> and with his wounds we are healed.
> All we like sheep have gone astray;
> we have turned—every one—to his own way;
> and the LORD has laid on him the iniquity of us all.[25]

As I read the passage to the women around the table, my heart swelled with gratitude, a flood of tears rushed to my eyes, my throat tightened, and I could barely choke out the words. "I don't know what has come over me," I said, noting their befuddled expressions. *How could I act so nutso in front of these women, some of whom I barely knew?*

What *had* come over me? Perhaps the better question is this: What had been *lifted* from me? Lifted was the sense of uselessness and grief that had hovered like a black cloud since I had lost so much

---

25.Isaiah 53:3-6

function in my arm. Lifted was the temptation to believe that this pain was serving no good purpose. Lifted was the notion that *I* was being chastened, afflicted and stricken by God. Lifted was the veil over my eyes that prevented me from seeing that in place of all this loss, God wanted to give me something so valuable that I would consider my sufferings not worth comparing with what He wanted to reveal.[26] What did He want to reveal? Himself—as the supreme Lover of my soul—as the One who considers *me* to have worth and value— so much so that He sacrificed His Son to redeem my undeserving soul from eternal wrath. It was immeasurably more than I could ever ask or even think of, but through this trial, God was revealing to me, in a way that I could *only now* really grasp, that His love for me knows no bounds, that there was nothing—no One—that He would spare for my sake. His plan from the beginning was that His Servant would suffer in my place—all so I could be in a right relationship with Him. *Amazing love! How can it be, that thou, my God, shouldst die for me?*[27]

A Micro Epilogue: It's been seven years since I was wheeled into the surgical suite where an amazing doctor cut the scar tissue and gave me back a fully functioning shoulder and arm. I don't often notice my scars, they're so tiny and a little faded, but when

---

26. Romans 8:18
27. "And Can It Be," a hymn by Charles Wesley, 1738

I do, I'm grateful for how they remind me of a certain moment under those glaring surgical lights: On the gurney, just before they knocked me out, a couple of nurses rolled me onto my right side, and strapped down my right hand; in the process, my gown fell open. By that point they had totally anesthetized my left arm, so I was helpless to pull it shut. I looked up and caught a nurse's eye. "I'm modest," I said to her with pleading eyes.

"You're covered," she said.

"No, *see?*" I said, looking down. I wouldn't blame her if she internally rolled her eyes, but she mercifully tugged my gown shut, undoubtedly thinking that in a minute, a lot more of me would be exposed. But it didn't matter. While I was conscious, I didn't want to be partially naked.

> And they crucified him and *divided his garments* among them, casting lots for them, to decide what each should take.[28]

*Total* nakedness, nine feet up, for all the world to see. We can hardly fathom how that felt. But my little scars and that moment on the gurney *compel* me to visualize it, and to receive the message of His love, of fellowship with Him, and joy in His presence, all over again.

Shortly after the surgery, I began thinking about the stories behind other people's scars. Certainly, God would be giving similar gifts to others in the midst of their suffering. Certainly, He'd be using

---

28.Mark 15:24, emphasis added.

their trials to reveal Himself more fully to His beloved sons and daughters. Yes and yes. Stories like these abound. Our faithful, wise, righteous, merciful and trustworthy Heavenly Father kindly brings storm clouds of blessings.

> You have multiplied, O LORD my God,
> your wondrous deeds and your thoughts toward us;
> none can compare with you!
> I will proclaim and tell of them,
> yet they are more than can be told.[29]

Nunc dimittis.

---

29. Psalm 40:5

Also available from Christian
Focus Publications...

'A wonderful antidote to self-pity' **Jennifer Rees Larcombe**

# Why Do Bad Things
## Happen to Good People?

M E L V I N   T I N K E R

ISBN 978-1-8579-2322-3

# Why Do Bad Things Happen to Good People?

# A Biblical Look at the problem of suffering

## MELVIN TINKER

Why is doing good no guarantee of an easy life? One of the most common objections to the Christian Faith is 'If God created the universe, and is still in control of it, then why does he allow suffering and injustice?' Melvin Tinker considers the different opinions people have before investigating the biblical answers about a crucial topic that needs to be faced by an evangelistic church. He looks at the situations biblical characters faced, the opposition to Jesus himself, and the suffering of the early church. This book provides the key factors behind the benefit and purpose of suffering.

*Right from the first page this book is easy reading, yet it deals with the most difficult subject Christians ever have to face—the question of why a loving God allows suffering. A wonderful antidote to self-pity, I can highly recommend this book to anyone, but particularly to those who struggle to know what to say or how to help when their friends are going through the mill.*

Jennifer Rees Larcombe
Christian Herald

A CHRISTIAN'S POCKET GUIDE TO

## SUFFERING

BRIAN H. COSBY

How God Shapes Us through Pain and Tragedy

ISBN 978-1-7819-1646-9

# A Christian's Pocket Guide to Suffering

## How God Shapes Us through Pain and Tragedy

### Brian H. Cosby

When tragedy strikes—the death of a child, hurricanes, a school shooting—we begin looking for an escape from the pain, a way out, or we clamor for answers from a panel of religious "experts" to explain the ever-present question, "Why?" We want answers and we want to believe that our suffering isn't meaningless. A Christian's Pocket Guide to Suffering seeks to simply, but clearly, present a biblical view of suffering so that your feet might land on the solid foundation of God's Word and the God of that Word and, there, find understanding and hope. All other ground is sinking sand.

*No matter who we are, suffering is something we'll encounter at some point in our lives, whether we're witness to someone else's pain and have no idea what to say or how to help, or dealing with our own sorrow and thinking no one else understands what we're going through. A Christian's Pocket Guide to Suffering by Brian H. Cosby is a relatively short read, but it's practical and Bible-centred, answering many of the questions we have about suffering, and pointing us to God's Word for hope in painful circumstances.*

Free Magazine

# Christian Focus Publications

Our mission statement –

STAYING FAITHFUL

In dependence upon God we seek to impact the world through literature faithful to His infallible Word, the Bible. Our aim is to ensure that the Lord Jesus Christ is presented as the only hope to obtain forgiveness of sin, live a useful life and look forward to heaven with Him.

Our books are published in four imprints:

## CHRISTIAN FOCUS

Popular works including biographies, commentaries, basic doctrine and Christian living.

## CHRISTIAN HERITAGE

Books representing some of the best material from the rich heritage of the church.

## MENTOR

Books written at a level suitable for Bible College and seminary students, pastors, and other serious readers. The imprint includes commentaries, doctrinal studies, examination of current issues and church history.

## CF4•K

Children's books for quality Bible teaching and for all age groups: Sunday school curriculum, puzzle and activity books; personal and family devotional titles, biographies and inspirational stories – because you are never too young to know Jesus!

Christian Focus Publications Ltd,
Geanies House, Fearn, Ross-shire,
IV20 1TW, Scotland, United Kingdom.
www.christianfocus.com
blog.christianfocus.com